Two Lifestyles, One Lifetime

An Inspiring Journey from Rock-Bottom Hopelessness to Wildly Extravagant Possibility

by Les Leventhal

as told to Barbie Levasseur

Two Lifestyles, One Lifetime

ISBN: 978-0692238080

For information, www.yogawithles.com

Book cover designed by Tony Kuehn, photography by Jennifer MacNiven Photography, and wardrobe provided by WE'AR. Photograph taken at Puri Wulundari, Ubud, Bali, Indonesia.

A special thanks to Barbie Levasseur.

* * *

For Joey

"Les Leventhal is a teacher for our modern times and speaks for all of us who have walked the irregular path. He is transparent, raw, funny, and completely honest about his own life experience and shares generously the tools that have enabled him to both survive and thrive. **Two Lifestyles, One Lifetime is an inspirational guide** that teaches us to embrace fully our own particular and – sometimes peculiar – life path without judgment or shame, and accept deeply and unapologetically each other and ourselves – exactly as we are. I highly recommend this book and know it can be of service to many."
– **SEANE CORN**, Yoga Teacher, Co-founder Off The Mat, Into The World

"Les' courageous introspection, unabashed honesty, and playful wit **breathe new life into age-old yoga philosophy**. He shares the teachings with authenticity and wisdom, the likes of which can only arise from intimate experiences, suffering, joy, desperation, hope, fall from grace, and redemption. A must read."
– **TIFFANY CRUIKSHANK**, L.Ac, MAOM, E-RYT

"*Two Lifestyles, One Lifetime* is a fantastic book containing an abundant wealth of honest information and inspiring knowledge. Les illustrates to us how in living these important ethical guidelines **we can transform our yoga practice beyond physical exercise to a complete and nurtured life practice**. Written by my friend and teacher, I cannot recommend this book highly enough."
– **MICHAEL BAIOCCHI**, founder of *Bala Yoga Studio*

"I know Les Leventhal as a friend and as a peer and as my teacher. I did not know Les Leventhal as a teenage alcoholic and prostitute. And this revelation makes his brilliance shine even brighter in my opinion. It is as if the lows have given a poignancy to the highs of his life now and the incredible darkness of his younger years has given greater definition to the incredible light that he now shares with the world through his yoga teaching. **Les has access to the causes of our suffering, because he himself has been deeply immersed in suffering.**"
– **ROGER RIPPY**, Co-Owner of YogaOne Studios, Director, Yoga Alliance

"Les has a special way of speaking from the heart and teaching directly from his life experiences to facilitate transformation in his students' lives. You gain the tools to transform through self inquiry. This physical experience manifests into a whole mind, body, and soul connection. Les teaches from a place of deep trust; **there is always so much joy with lightness and freedom in the way he connects his students to their higher self**. A true master that shines the light bright, for anyone who needs to find their way."
– **TINA TAINUI**, Yoga Teacher, Melbourne, Australia

DEDICATION

The original title of this book was, *Got a Life, Go Fish.* I don't want to flippantly wish the reader good luck. This is the story of a lot of my life. While I recognize not everyone gets to have a life or gets to have choice in their life or may have a shortened life, I think it is important to receive a message of hope, trust, and faith in something. To pull us up out of the depths of despair even when our very own souls appear to have abandoned us in our time of need. So, for those of us who have known struggle, heartbreak, addiction, or abuse of any kind from others or from ourselves, I wrote this book for us, so that we can unite in hope for a brighter day and help others who come after us. I promise if you reach out and ask for help, and offer some help when it seems like you have nothing to give, there will be a hand reaching back always, in ways that we could not even begin to have imagined. A healing love will very quietly and gently rebuild a life worth living. For those of you who have not had this experience in your life, I hope that this book gives you some of the signs of something coming and to seek love and support so you don't have to stray as far as I did. And look around, there's someone nearby who needs your shoulder to lean on right now.

CONTENTS

ACKNOWLEDGEMENTS

I walked through the door in desperate humiliation – I continue walking the path with all of you in humility.

I just felt a few more words were necessary because so much has changed since real attention was turned towards this book. So many people have put so many hours into helping me and making me realize a dream, which is to continue to notice when I take the seat of selfishness and am guided back towards selflessness.

There are so many intentions for this book. Originally, it was meant to reach out to young, gay, male, runaway, addicts and then I thought – wait, I wasn't reading back then and now, it's for everyone seeking anything. In no way is the book meant to make anyone responsible for the directions, paths, and alleys I chose and still choose to wander. Instead, it is meant to be a beacon of light and hope that someday we can all see that life shows up exactly as we need, which I firmly believe comes from karma and this very precious opportunity to take responsibility and stay in loving relationship with ourselves and others – yeah that's my aim if I had to say I have an aim and goal today. It's my codependency that would love for this tool to help prevent some from suffering, but I know that's up to the infinite wisdom of this life. So, that means, I would like for some of the readers to know, you are not alone, ever.

A very big thank you, and bow, and debt of gratitude to Barbie Levasseur for sitting with me for so many hours and laughing with me at things that, for some of you, are so not laughable and also for allowing me to sit in public at Samovar and cry. Thank you to Eric Gillespie, my assistant in San Francisco, for many years, who lived a portion of this book with me and watched me turn and spin on occasion; and grow up a little bit in this world we live in and practice yoga and recovery on and off the mat. To Amber Hoffman, my new assistant in Bali, who has been a lifesaver; just when I was praying for guidance, support, and help – poof! You arrived.

To my many friends and family who have seen me through and felt the depths of despair and prayed for me when I couldn't pray at all, thank you. Without all of you to remind me that I am garden variety, a birth, a life, and a death just like those who have blazed trails before us so that we could have this experience, I would have already died of the isolation. So, thank you, Honey Hogan, for holding my hand and guiding me gently when needed, Richard Ceely for picking up the phone in quite possibly the most desperate moment of my life, and Basil Green, for taking a hold of love in transition that held dark and light. This paragraph could go on forever, especially because I don't follow grammar rules when I write – so, I will conclude with one final dedication.

To the men that tried to love me, thank you for trying to show me something I so wanted and was also so terrified of. To those of you who have already passed on from this life and you might have felt used and abused, I didn't know, but I do now. Finally, for my eternal love – Mr. Joe Thompson – Joey – You made a choice to see me through the thick, the thin, and the very thin – it still baffles me some days that our love is 15 years young and old, tested, and weathered. You are everything to and for me and I know we're not spring chickadees but I still wonder what it would be like to adopt a couple of children with you and grow a love and family in a way that would be so challenging, I think, and so rewarding for them, I hope. There isn't anything (besides cleaning house) I wouldn't do for you to help you realize your dreams. I am the luckiest man in the world to have you, to be able to tell you anything and to only receive love in return – you showed me that love is for everyone. That you saw something in me when my life was turning from dim to dark again is still beyond my comprehension but within my humble sphere of gratitude. You are such a tremendous part of my second lifestyle in this one lifetime.

It's a day like today that I feel complete and empty all at the same time as I know that I've had more than my fair share of life and love and yet I was recently reminded to keep going forward, keep dreaming. Thank you all and thank you God, that truth and love in all things.

FOREWORD

by Darren Main

Every spiritual tradition from every culture has a moral code by which its participants aspire to live, and yoga is no exception. Just as Christians and Jews rely on the Ten Commandments to provide a moral compass, yogis have the *yamas* and the *niyamas* to guide their behavior and lifestyle choices.

On the surface these precepts seem straightforward enough - non-harming, truthfulness and so on, but a closer look by an honest spiritual seeker reveals a very uncomfortable truth. Simply put, "Easier said than done."

It is easy to be honest when the stakes are not high, to have faith in a Higher Power when things are going your way, or to practice sexual moderation when your libido feels more like a sleeping kitten rather than a prowling tiger.

Yet, there are times in all of our lives when following the principles set forth in the *yamas* and *niyamas* can seem daunting and impossible. It is also why so many books on yoga philosophy can feel like tomes on ashram life rather than practical guides for modern yogis.

Les Leventhal is the perfect person to write about the

yamas and the *niyamas* – not because he has mastered them, but because he has lived them. In *Two Lifestyles, One Lifetime: An Inspiring Journey from Rock-Bottom Hopelessness to Wildly Extravagant Possibility*, Les shares so openly and honestly about his struggles as well as his success that living the *yamas* and *niyamas* feels real, attainable and most importantly, relevant.

Because so many religious and spiritual traditions advocate an absolute view of morality, seekers may often throw up their hands in frustration. Les takes a very different approach, which is both refreshing and inspiring. His raw unbridled candor gives all of us permission to stumble and fall. More importantly Les' words inspire us to get back up again, and again and again.

Les uses his own inspirational life story to demonstrate that the practice of yoga generally, and the *yamas* and *niyamas* specifically, are not about the number of times you miss the mark, but rather about the number of times you take the shot knowing full well you may miss again. And you don't need to look any further than Les' life to see that it works.

While the details of Les' amazing journey may be very different from the details of your own, you are sure to relate to this book because his struggles and successes are so universal, so human, and so familiar. There is nothing peachy about this book and that is what makes its voice seem so near. You are sure to find yourself nodding your head as you relate even if you can barely imagine what it was like. At times, as you read these pages, you may laugh, at other times you may find yourself brushing tears from your cheeks, but in the wake of this story, you will find countless nuggets of truth, wisdom and inspiration.

Yoga was meant to be lived. Even as many scholars have tried to keep this ancient practice locked away in the vault of philosophical discourse, it remains a practice designed to help us make more mindful choices, to live with more awareness and to achieve *moksha* or liberation from all that binds our minds and holds us hostage.

In the same way that an addict finds strength and hope in hearing the stories of other addicts, Les' story will give seasoned yogis, those new to the path and those who have yet to begin, a much needed dose of strength and hope.

So journey with Les from his early life as a gay sex-worker, through his drug addiction and recovery, to finding yoga and eventually to becoming one of the most influential yoga teachers in the modern world. Those who know Les will not be surprised by his open heart and raw honesty as they read these pages, and those who do not know Les personally, will feel like they do by simply turning the pages of this book. But more importantly, you will come to know yourself through hearing his story.

– **DARREN MAIN**, author of *Yoga and the Path of the Urban Mystic*

INTRODUCTION
by Barbie Levasseur

Les and I could not have lived our twenties more differently. While he was getting high, partying, and prostituting, I was finishing college, teaching yoga, and I've still never even tried a cigarette. However, few other teachers' words have resounded with me as deeply as have his. That's the power of Les' teaching: rather than speak about how we live our lives on the outside – a mere symptom of our internal landscape – he speaks to the profoundly human tendencies we all navigate. Drawing on wisdom from his own experience, he challenges students to notice their addictions (if not alcohol and drugs, then food? Sex? Shopping? Even yoga?), probe their insecurities, and meet their fears ("Quit your job," he often suggests playfully).

When I first practiced with Les, I was keeping a journal of what I learned from the various classes I attended. My entries for most teachers' classes consisted of several sketches of interesting poses and maybe one creative cue. Les is known for his rich, juicy, variation-packed sequencing, and more than any other teacher I've practiced with, he empowers students to do things they didn't think were possible. However, what set my entries about his classes apart from the others was how many quotations from him I wrote down.

· "Lower down from plank for a count of five... four... three... two... one – 'One' is not down. 'One' is the teacher of desire."
· "Only 652,326 more."
· "See if you can back out for the last couple breaths to savor the posture. We're always right on the edge, but if you step back from the edge you can enjoy the view."
· "In case you're wondering, you're doing the right thing."
· "Every practice I change one thing, and that's everything."
· "One day you'll lay down to rest in your final corpse pose. Every time you get up, it's another chance at life."

Taken at face value, all of his insightful statements teach students how to practice *asana* (poses) gracefully and how to reap the full benefits of that practice. The deeper message is a challenge to apply all of that *svadhyaya* (self-study) off the mat. When in your life do *tapas* (discipline) and grace give way to desire? How would your choices change if you aspired for long term sustainability rather than bearing down to reach a goal? Where are you so driven to achieve that you undermine the benefits of achievement? How is self-judgment and insecurity blocking *santosha* (contentment) in your daily actions? What in your life is habitual and stagnant? Who would you call, hug, apologize to, forgive, or love if you knew you were minutes from that final *savasana* (corpse pose)? Instead of answering these questions for his students, Les empowers people to unearth the answers for themselves through embodiment, intuition, and self-study.

When I began an apprenticeship with Les to develop my own expression as a yoga instructor, I noticed that unlike teachers who put on airs of otherworldliness and equanimity, Les shows he's alongside his students rather than above them, by being genuine and sharing his challenges. This is one of the reasons he gets through to people. Rather than responding to his challenges with frustration or aversion, he talks about them as one might a dear friend: with love and *karuna* (compassion). His message is: it's okay to be human. It's okay to feel. It's okay to have a past. It's all okay. When a student jumps back to *chaturanga* (low push-up) by force of habit when the cue was to step forward into *uttanasana* (forward fold), Les often thanks them for their unique contribution to class. If a student stands up into *utkatasana* (chair pose) instead of *urdhva hastasana* (upward salute), Les accepts it as a special request. Sometimes he teases, "Don't anticipate," to bring students' unconscious tendencies into consciousness. This attitude helps students begin to see that their mistakes are not shameful acts that they should hide from others, but beautiful, essential events that are an unparalleled opportunity for self-study, learning, and transformation.

This idea that everyone is okay wherever they are underlies the multitude of variations Les includes in his classes. It's a staple for him to say, "We all have different gifts and challenges." He tells students that he offers such a variety of poses and advanced variations so that everyone has an option to experience their gifts, and more importantly, so everyone – even seasoned practitioners – can experience challenge. Typically, yoga studios categorize their classes on a scale of Level One to Level Three; Les often says, "I teach an All Levels class. That means levels one, two, three... four, five, six... seven, eight, nine... ten... eleven." Although he encourages people to try everything, they never have to keep doing things that don't work for their bodies. He says, "This class is a breakfast buffet. Take what you want. Put what you don't want back on the buffet table with a bite taken out of it."

One sunny Friday afternoon, I ran into a friend while attending Les' class, and afterwards we walked out together. She'd been practicing with Les via his online videos since long before she moved to San Francisco, so she was thrilled to now be able to take his class in-person on a regular basis. She shared my feelings that Les' way of expressing concepts in and around yoga profoundly resonated with her. "I could listen to him talk all day. Why hasn't he written a book? I would totally read a book about what he's been through," she said. "I've heard he's been to jail. Do you know if he's been to jail?" At that time, I didn't have answers to any of those questions for her.

The next time I saw Les, I asked him if he'd ever considered writing a book. "Yes, actually," he said, "Right after I quit my job at the bank, I wrote down the outline for a book about my journey. The only problem," he continued, "is that I'm not a writer. I guess I'd need to find a ghostwriter or something like that."

"I'll be your ghostwriter," I blurted out. I wasn't a writer by trade. I'd written essays and blogged, but I'd never written anything as long as a book. I'd been practicing with Les for a while, though, and as I mentioned, he relentlessly empowers people to step into their fear and do things they didn't think possible.

The next week he brought me a typed page dated April 5th, 2005. The title was *"Got a Life – Go Fish!"* followed by the subtitle, *"The Longest Route from A to B – Confusing Perceived Success with Your Own Identity."* It included a short dedication and a list of quirky chapter titles followed by brief handwritten notes about what each chapter was about. From there we got to work.

The words in this book are Les' own, pulled from hours upon hours of interviews in the back room of Samovar Tea Lounge in San Francisco (during which I learned the answer to my friend's question about jail). The way Les tells stories made such an impact on me throughout my practice with him, so as a writer I preserved his voice as much as possible to share that experience with readers. As one of Les' students, it was such a rich experience to write Les' memoir and vicariously experience the back-story that makes everything he teaches authentic.

While collaborating on the book, Les and I had many memorable conversations about what to leave in and what to edit out. We changed many of the names due to the sensitivity of the subject, and we had an ongoing conversation about the harsh language. The most vulgar words Les says in his yoga classes are "bum-bum" and "caca-asana" – a stark contrast to time periods described in the book when he was known for his inability to get through two sentences without profanity. He found the swearing in the book jarring and had some fear about how it would be received, so we softened the language. Les moved to Bali while we were in the final stages of editing, and the last time I saw him he said, "If I die before we publish the book, change all the names back, put all the f-bombs back in, and get it published." By the final edit of the manuscript, we injected the fearlessness and authenticity behind that statement back into the book. Les came from a place that was gritty, crass, and even violent at times, and we wanted to share that with *sauca* (purity) even if the effect was raw and edgy.

During my final refinements of *Two Lifestyles, One Lifetime*, I mentioned offhandedly to another yoga teacher that I often practiced with Les. "Don't you think that being a big-time yoga teacher has kind of gone to his head?" she asked, referring to his infectious charisma, his radiating personality, and his flair for drama. "Oh no," I laughed, thinking back over the manuscript I had now read over, and over, and over, "Success didn't get to his head, he's always been like that. If anything, teaching yoga has softened him." I thought more about the choices Les has made throughout his lifetime, then added, "And given his personality, I think sharing yoga is one of the most amazing things he could be doing."

PART I: SATYA

Is it lying to say "I know" when it really should be "I think?"
Are the effects of lying by omission as harmful as lying with
words? How would speaking your truth affect your
relationship with yourself and with others?

Let's Dance

It was August fourth, 1985, 7:48 p.m., and seventy-eight degrees outside when my plane touched down in Los Angeles. As the captain relayed some of these numbers over the intercom, their relationship struck me. It was as if the universe was sending me a message that this would be different from every other time I'd run away. Everything would come together. At the time, I didn't trust anyone or anything, but for whatever reason I had faith that this place would be my salvation. At seventeen, I couldn't yet predict that this place, these people, would be any different from those I'd left behind. I couldn't foresee that the cycle of insanity that I'd been living my whole life wouldn't stop or slow down; it would spin wildly out of control.

As the plane slowly taxied to the gate, I alternated between primping hair and adjusting and readjusting the volume of my walkman. *Did I get away with it?* I wondered anxiously. In my head, I replayed the desperate phone call that got me my seat on the plane.

* * *

"Good Morning, thank you for – "

I cut the Trans World Airlines receptionist off before she could complete her greeting, "My name is Les Leventhal and my dad's name is Lee Leventhal. He was in a horrible car accident and is in a coma at Cedars-Sinai Hospital. I need to be on the next plane from Indianapolis to Los Angeles." I gasped, "I need to – to – ," my sentence was stifled by a half-concealed sob.

"Let me see what we have available," she replied professionally.

"I need to get there today" I implored, "It's really bad. They called me and said it's really bad. Oh God. This can't be happening." I started crying harder.

"Okay, I'm looking up available flights," she said in a reassuring tone. She put me on hold for a minute or two. I rolled my eyes when the sickly soothing elevator music clicked on, and held the phone away from my ear. I snapped back into character when she came back on the line and said, "The only seats we have available today are business class. Will that be okay?"

"Yes. I have to be on this flight. I don't care about the cost; I just need to get to LA. What time do I need to be at the airport?"

"To get on the next flight you'll have to be there in three hours. Or, there's another flight tomorrow morning that I could – "

"I'll be there in three hours" I interrupted, gripping the phone between my shoulder and crocodile-tear-stained cheek, while beginning to stuff clothes into my duffel bag.

She quickly finished booking the flight for me. I hung up the phone and scrawled a note to my dad: "I realized I lied. Sorry. Didn't mean to lie. Can't follow your rules." Leaving the note beside the phone, I slid my dad's credit card and some cash I'd stolen from his wallet into the side pocket of my duffel bag and marched resolutely out the front door.

* * *

I felt my shoulders move away from the seat back as the plane came to a halt. I exhaled. Maybe for the first time in my life. I'd dreamed for months of arriving in Los Angeles, and now only a pane of clear acrylic plastic separated me from the warm California sun sitting low in the sky.

When the aisle cleared, I stood up in my pec-hugging T-shirt, tight-as-hell jeans, and sleek mahogany cowboy boots, and slung my half-empty canvas duffel bag over one shoulder. It was filled with more hair products than clothes. I was a bleached blonde. I had big hair, a big hair dryer, and lots of gel, mousse, and shampoo. I had only twenty-eight dollars in my pocket. That's how I showed up in LA.

Sweet Sweet Fantasy, Baby

I stepped out of the airport into a California evening. I closed my eyes and inhaled, enjoying the dry air that filled my lungs. The weather was warm but not humid. I thought, *I don't know what this is going to be*. Although LA had several draws, when I ran away, I wasn't focused on going somewhere, I was focused on leaving. Escaping my problems. I thought I'd figure out the solutions once I got away.

The first thing I did was head to Bar One on Melrose Avenue, which I'd seen advertised in a porn magazine. One of my sexy gay boy mags had drawn me to California in the first place; there was a spread featuring a hot bleached blonde surfer. On the first page, he was in a striped bikini. He had a beautiful body, perfect hair, sweet face, blue eyes. Then I turned the page and it got even better. The blurb next to his bare bronzed body talked about his gymnastics days, how he was putting himself through UCLA, and how he spent every day at the beach. Later, I would learn that the biographies they print about porn stars are mostly fabricated, specifically designed to seduce men like me to continue buying magazines and videos; but at the time, I believed the smart, sexy, sculpted guy from my magazine was living my ideal life in Los Angeles.

* * *

Even from a young age, besides defying my parents, nothing affected my decision-making more than pursuing a hot guy. In fourth grade, I decided to play alto saxophone in band class just to have something in common with Donald Von Hagen, the first chair alto sax player in the seventh grade. In spite of the fact that students don't skip grades in band, my fantasy was, *I'm going to play alto sax and sit next to him.*

As a preteen living with my mom in New York, I never fit in. I always knew that I was different, and I had already begun to explore the hidden part of myself that longed to be expressed. I used to have friends over, and we'd play strip poker. Some of them were into it; some were disgusted at the suggestion. The farthest I went with my friends was pretending that one of us was Lee Majors and the other was Farrah Fawcett. I wanted more, but somehow I knew I had to keep my needs and true desires hidden from everyone I knew. Internally, I had acceptance; I'd always been comfortable with being gay. What I didn't have was a way of being in the world with it. I was always looking for a place where I could feel safe to explore who I was.

When I was about twelve, I began secretly exploring some of the seedier places that gay men could go to play. Before the Internet was widespread, you'd find out about these places by stumbling across them accidentally or by following a note scrawled on a bathroom wall. One of my favorite places to go was the Macy's bathroom. Using the money from my paper route to pay for bus fare, I went there frequently and would stay for hours at a time. It was like an addiction for me, my first one.

I used to see the same people over and over again. Many of them had no problem having sex with a boy my age, either right there in the bathroom or in a woodsy area nearby. One old guy brought me into a cigarette-smoke-filled van where he clearly lived. After we slept together, he paid me five dollars and sent me on my way. That was my first time getting paid for sex. Thank God for inflation. Looking back, I think, *Woodsy areas? Vans? That could have ended so much worse than it did.*

There was a guy who had long hair and always wore tight brand-new-blue Levis and slinky shirts and was constantly in the Macy's bathroom. He would go into one of the stalls, hang out, smoke, and wait for guys to come in so he could play with them. One time, as I was about to push open the bathroom door, he came out soaking wet. The Macy's employees had gotten above the stall he was in, pulled out a ceiling tile, and dumped a bucket of water on him to try to deter him from coming back. The message I received was: *This is what you get.* I was having thoughts about being gay, I was acting on them, and the advisory was loud and clear: *Don't tell anyone. You will be humiliated. Here's a great example.*

* * *

Once I got to Bar One in Los Angeles, I was disappointed to find out my fake ID didn't fly with the broad-shouldered bouncer. After a spirited but unsuccessful attempt to charm my way past the burly man, I resigned myself to sitting outside the bar, my stomach growling. As men walked past me and pulled open the bar door I was enveloped by the sounds of laughter and chatter accompanied by an upbeat snippet of Madonna or Wham! Then, as the door thudded shut the sounds of the Melrose Avenue traffic muted the sounds of the party inside. Sitting on my duffel bag, I looked like a lost homeless kid who needed something. And I did – I felt so alone, thinking, *Wow, I don't know where I'm sleeping tonight.*

Every now and then I'd see a friendly face, and I'd smile, "Hi, how are you?" Some of them would smile back politely and then quickly look away before continuing into the bar. Some of them would just look me up and down judgmentally. Some would completely ignore my existence. Every interaction was humiliating, feeding into my self-consciousness: *What must they think of me? They must think I'm really bad. They must think I'm awful.*

Bar One seemed like a hotspot for prostitution. Sitting outside the door that night, that's how the men there saw me – as one of *them*, someone working the street. And, I mean, I was, really. I wasn't ready to admit it to myself, but that was exactly what I was doing. I had a New York upbringing. I had street smarts and knew how to land on my feet. Somehow I knew that if I sat outside of that bar things would work out. I knew some guy would come pick me up. And some guy did: around midnight, a man came out of the bar and wandered over to me: "So, where are you from?"

"Uh, the East coast," I said, looking up at him. He was cute.

"How long have you lived out here?"

"Mmm, since today. I'm kind of moving out here."

"Ah, I see," he laughed. "You look like you need a place to sleep. And a meal."

I smiled weakly, "Is it that obvious?"

"Yeah, kinda," he laughed, "And I'm guessing you have no money."

I touched my pocket and tried to remember how much of my twenty-eight dollars I'd given the cabbie, "No, not really."

"Come on," he offered his hand to help me up, "You can spend the night with me." I knew that this meant sleeping in his bed, not on his couch, but I was okay with that. I gripped his hand as if shaking on a business deal, and he pulled me to my feet.

With everything I owned in my two bags, I climbed into his car, and he drove me up the Hollywood Freeway to his house in the valley. Sitting in his kitchen as he made me a sandwich, I thought, *Nice place. Nice, cute guy. What are the chances? I'm letting this guy do whatever he wants.* I told myself I would have totally slept with him under other circumstances, even if I didn't need him for food and shelter. I told myself it was just icing on the cake that he was helping me out in exchange for sex.

After breakfast the next morning the man said, "So, you can't stay in my house all day, I have to work. Where do you want to go?" I thought for a moment, "Um, just drop me on Sunset Boulevard in West Hollywood." I'd written down the address for Jockster Magazine, the porn magazine in which my UCLA gymnast had been featured.

Before I left for Los Angeles, I don't remember consciously thinking, *I'm going to LA to do porn,* but deep down I must have known that's what I was headed for. Why else would I have written down that address? At that time, I was so used to lying to everyone around me that I couldn't even be truthful with myself.

Satya

The Yoga Sutras of Patanjali are verses that form an ancient text outlining yoga philosophy. The sutras describe five hindrances (*yamas*) and five observances (*niyamas*) for balanced living.

These are:

Yamas:

Ahimsa: Non-violence

Satya: Truthfulness

Asteya: Non-stealing

Brahmacharya: Sexual responsibility

Aparigraha: Non-greed

Niyamas:

Sauca: Cleanliness

Santosha: Contentment

Tapas: Austerity

Svadhyaya: Self-study

Isvara Pranidhana: Surrender of the self to God.

The *yamas* are mainly about how we relate to others, and the *niyamas* are mainly about how we relate to ourselves. However, how we treat ourselves and allow ourselves to be treated trickles over into how we treat others; and, how we treat others affects how we allow ourselves to be treated. For example, we may lie to others because we assume others are lying to us. In turn, we assume others are untrustworthy because we ourselves aren't to be trusted.

Some yoga teachers understand the *yamas* and *niyamas* as clearly defined principles. They can say, "This is what they are. Period. End of story." That's not how I understand them. The idea that there is only one way, one path, that's not yoga for me. The *ya*'s and *niya*'s give us direction and guidance, but each of us must discover, interpret, and explore these principles for ourselves.

It may already be clear that as a young adult I was out of touch with the *yamas* and *niyamas*. I was unwilling to submit to any authority, let alone God. I was so discontent with my life that my greed for something different drove me to lie and steal to get to Los Angeles. Once there, I manipulated people with sex to get what I wanted. Many people who meet me as a yoga teacher now have a hard time believing that I could have come from a place of such carelessness. But, as I say in my yoga classes, "Sometimes in order to find balance, you have to lose it." In order to understand what it is to be non-harming, we have to experience what it is like to harm or to be harmed. To understand what it is to live with integrity, we have to live in hypocrisy.

Yoga and meditation are all about self-study and awareness. As we observe our relationships with others and with ourselves, we will gradually realize that we have to live our lives in a certain way to avoid self-contradiction. I've lived my life as a hypocrite. Many people have known me in that way, and some still do. And, I will be a hypocrite again, even though I practice yoga and meditate daily. I'm going to overstep others' boundaries, fueled by my own doubt, self-loathing, and fear. We are human, which means we can practice the *yamas* and *niyamas,* but may never quite perfect them. Every time we topple over, falter, misstep, it's an opportunity to learn and to grow.

Had I shared my story when I was seventeen, or in my twenties, or even when I first conceived the outline for this book in my thirties, it would have come out far different. When I was a teen, I wasn't even honest enough to tell myself the truth, let alone anyone else. I was adept at identifying what people wanted to hear, and telling them that. It has taken a consistent practice of *satya,* truthfulness, for me to learn to speak honestly instead.

Now, I am in a better place to answer peoples' questions about my life, about prostitution or drug addiction. I don't have to dance around it, sugar-coat it, or make up a story anymore. I know I'm putting myself out there, and that's okay.

Les Leventhal

PART II: ASTEYA

Do you steal from others? If not objects, do you steal time? Affection? Self-esteem? What void within yourself are you trying to fill with what you've taken from others? What is it that you actually need in order to heal?

Let's Get Physical. Or Not

After my first night in Los Angeles, the guy from Bar One dropped me off a few blocks away from the Jockster Magazine office. I paused briefly outside the door, then, I swallowed my nervousness, stood up tall, and strode in with conviction. The man at reception, who would later introduce himself as Jack, had a plain face, long shaggy brown hair, and a great tan like everyone else in LA. He looked up from his desk and started laughing.

"Hi," I said, hesitantly.

"Ugh, another one," Jack scoffed, as if gossiping with someone else in the room.

I cleared my throat, broadened my chest as much as possible, and said confidently, "I'm your next model."

"You *all* are," he laughed, "You guys are a dime a dozen. Please, you are so not of age. Whatever. How did you get here and where are you from?"

My eyes welled up.

"Oh honey," Jack smiled, softening his sarcastic tone slightly, "You're another one, another run away. You're from New York, aren't you?"

"Originally, yeah," I sniffled.

"So, how underage are you?" he probed.

"I'm not!" I protested, "I have my ID right here." I pulled out my wallet.

"Let me see." He took the card from my hands and studied it for less than a second, "This is fake. It's about as real as your hair color."

"Fuck you, it's not fake." The tears started flowing again. "I'm eighteen."

"Oh yeah, what year were you born?"

"I don't know. I'm a high school dropout, I can't do math," I said, smirking through tears.

He laughed, "That's good. I haven't heard that one before." He thought for a moment, "Listen, I'm going to introduce you to the owner, the guy who chooses everybody, but that ID's not going to fly. I'm sure you'll be coming back when you're of legal age."

"I *am* of legal age," I called after him as he left the room.

Jack sent me back to meet Carson, the guy responsible for recruiting models. He was tall with icy blue eyes and silky smooth blonde hair, cut short and parted to the side. He had a v-neck t-shirt on, and no evidence of chest hair, just sexy tanned skin I wanted to get my hands all over. I immediately thought, *Ah, I can fuck my way through this, no problem. This'll be really easy.* But he turned down my advances, "Nah, sorry, I have a boyfriend. And, I don't really mess around with the models."

I smiled, "You haven't met me yet." Now I had a goal.

I took my clothes off, took a few pictures, and he said, "We'll be in touch."

I paused in the lobby on my way out. Jack studied me for a moment. "So where are you going now?" he asked.

"I don't know," I said slowly.

"Do you even know where you are?"

"Um, I think Santa Monica Boulevard is down that way," I said, waving my hand in an arc.

"What? Are you going to go out on the street and work?" Santa Monica Boulevard was well known for prostitution.

"I don't have a job."

"I'm guessing you don't have any place to sleep and probably need one," he said looking me up and down

17

with apparent judgment. "Who knows where you were last night."

"I just got to town last night," I snapped back.

"That's what everybody says," he smiled playfully.

"It's true," I insisted.

He continued, "You can stay at my place for a few days. I have family coming into town this weekend, so you'll have to figure something else out by then, but yeah, you can stay for a few days."

I stared at him in disbelief.

"Here's the key to my house," he said, "It's like, three blocks from here. Stay there. Just go relax for the afternoon. My refrigerator's full. There's a pool at my complex if you want to go for a swim. Just relax. And whatever you've got going on, don't worry."

I took the key from him slowly. "Uh, thank you," I stuttered, not knowing what to make of his blind trust.

He gave me directions, and said, "Go home, take a shower, get some food, and I'll be there in a couple of hours, and we'll chat. You're not going to get a job here just yet, but maybe I can help you out." Then, just as I was about to walk out the door, he added seriously, "If you rob me, I'll come find you." He said it in a way that made me believe he would.

Jack lived a block from all the most popular West Hollywood nightlife spots. The Rage was a bar I'd seen advertised in porn magazines. Studio One was a disco club that I would find out I could sneak into occasionally. That area was two straight blocks of high-maintenance, overly-tanned, overly-made-up, plastic-surgeried queens. I fit right in.

After walking around a bit, I went to Jack's place, and did exactly what he told me to do. I was normally a snoop and a thief, but I didn't nose around or steal anything, I just relaxed. It wasn't out of respect or appreciation. It was because I knew this was all I had. I didn't want to get kicked out. Looking back now, I owe my life to him. I got so lucky in my first twenty-four hours in California. I met two men who were much kinder than I was at the time.

A few hours later, Jack walked in the door and laughed to see me sprawled out on the couch watching Days of Our Lives. "I'm assuming you don't know how to cook," he said.

"No, not really," I admitted.

"Okay, I'll make dinner," he said, and fired up the barbecue by the pool.

As he cooked, we had a frank conversation about who I was and where I came from.

Le Divorce

I told Jack about how I'd spent my whole life trying to escape my parents' non-stop cycle of screaming, door-slamming, leaving, and coming back. My dad, a big guy, 5'5 by 5'5 in all directions, was constantly busy with work affairs and love affairs. In response to my dad's misdoings, not to mention mine, my mom frequently played the victim, earning our pity and guilt.

Looking back, I think they did the best job they could with the information they had about being parents, being in a relationship, being married, and then being divorced. They took care of me in terms of food and shelter, but I was left wanting for love and affection. Maybe it was there, and it just wasn't the right flavor, kind, or size. My solution was: whatever my parents said, "Don't do," I did. If it was something kids weren't supposed to do, something the adults reserved for themselves, I knew it had to be fun. When I got caught – and I always got caught – my mom would scream at me angrily, sob about her own feelings of shortcomings as a parent, and slap me with a guilt trip or with the back of her hand. At that time, there wasn't much information available about the long-term negative effects of physical punishment. One time my mom even clocked me with a frying pan. In truth, I would simultaneously hate her and bask in the glow of her full, undivided attention.

I was always in trouble at school too. It wasn't enough to be a kid among other kids. I was smart enough that I was capable of getting the best marks in the class, but sometimes I would purposely fail stuff to get my teachers to raise an eyebrow. I also had a filthy mouth, which I learned from my parents. And, that wasn't the only thing I picked up from them. Once, I shoved a girl, who called me fat, so hard it sent her back end through the low window we were standing next to, shattering it. I got sent out into the hall frequently, where I was told to keep quiet and stay on the black line near the wall – instructions I disobeyed without fail. Occasionally, I'd end up in detention, and when I pushed that girl through the window they called my mom in for a meeting, but my grades were good enough that I never got in any real trouble.

I told Jack about the first time I ran away from home when I was seven, before my parents got divorced. I left with nothing but six dollars, my stuffed koala bear, and the keys to my house. My friend Matthew and I plotted to leave and never go back. Well, that wasn't quite true. We planned to get pink bubblegum ice cream at Baskin Robbins and go see a movie. Then, after everyone was asleep, we were going to sneak back into our houses and rob them. *Then* we'd leave and never go back.

We made it to the movie theater and we were sure we'd fooled the attendants when they let us into an R-rated movie. Little did we know that after they let us in, they began calling around to police stations to see if anyone had reported missing kids.

When the lights went down in the theater that evening, the darkness and solitude calmed me. Finally, I had some relief from the insanity at home – the fear, the doubt, the low self-esteem. It was the same way I would feel using drugs later in life. It was a numbing, an escape, and a break. One thing was always the same though: when the high wore off, nothing had changed.

When we walked out of the movie theater, the police were there, waiting for us. We were busted. At least they didn't put me in handcuffs for the squad car ride. Not this time, anyway.

That night, my mom pummeled me with guilt trip after guilt trip until I felt awful. She and my dad were going to have the canals dragged for fear I'd fallen in. My mom asked me what the hell I had been thinking and implored me to tell her what she and my dad had done wrong as parents. When tears started streaming down my cheeks, she told me to cut it out. I didn't stop. "Stop crying or else," she warned. I was always curious if *or else* would mean something different this time. It never did. She smacked me, told me I was grounded, and sent me off to my room, where my dad, who was exceptionally skilled with a belt, was waiting. He was especially skilled that night.

I felt terrible. But I didn't admit to Jack that it was a beautiful wonderful kind of terrible. My mother's anger nurtured my deep-seated desire for my parents' attention. Being grounded meant I would have someone there to watch over me or to call to make sure I was being good and doing what I was supposed to do. Being grounded meant I was guaranteed to continue getting attention. Looking back, that was my first drug: attention. I felt a lack of affection, and I filled that void any way I could. It didn't matter what kind of attention I got: good or bad, I craved it, I longed for it, I lived for it.

My parents finally split for good when I was ten. When they called my sister and me downstairs to tell us they were separating, we thought we were in trouble. My dad was in the big recliner we had, rocking back and forth, crying. He loved to put on a show. My mom was the one who broke the news. She went on to assure us it had nothing to do with us and that we'd still see both of them. Then she looked us each in the eye and said, "But, we haven't told anyone else in the family, and we don't want you to tell your friends. Don't tell anybody." My throat tightened immediately. The truth was a secret. They wanted to save face and keep looking good on the outside. I don't know who they thought they were kidding. Their arguments would get so loud sometimes that my friends who lived nearby would ask me about them the next day.

The morning after my parents announced their separation to us, all the neighborhood kids went out to the bus stop half an hour early to play kick ball like we always did before school. I felt different, isolated. I had no one to talk to about what I was going through. I had no one to trust.

My dad always said, "You don't tell people what's going on because then they can use it against you," which is the opposite of how I live my life now. I tell everyone what's going on so I can get help and support.

When someone asks me, "How are you doing?" instead of replying on impulse with, "Fine, thank you," I practice *satya*, truthfulness. I take a moment to check in and tell the person who's asking how I'm actually doing. Because I trust people enough that I answer this question honestly, my life is now filled with people who actually care about my answer. Addiction – whether it's to food, drugs, sex, or gambling – is a disease of isolation. Yoga and recovery is all about communities, connecting, and uniting. *Satya* and the other *yamas* are the foundation of interacting with others. Without them, we shut others out, push them away, and block any chance of authentically sharing our lives and experiences with others.

In the Yoga Sutras, truthfulness is more than a moral principle that allows us to build community. Patanjali writes that once someone has firmly established a practice of *satya*, they gain control of reality; what they say must come true, because they only speak the truth (Yoga Sutras verse 2.36). A habit of dishonesty doesn't just break other peoples' trust, it renders us powerless. We teach ourselves that our intentions have nothing to do with how reality unfolds. It wasn't until I was able to be truthful, to myself and to others, about the sources of my *dukkha*, suffering, that I was able to begin to move beyond that suffering. There was a big steaming pile of *dukkha* in my life by the time I was willing to acknowledge it.

Goin' Back to Indiana

As we ate dinner, I told Jack about how after the divorce my dad stayed on Long Island close to our family, but when I was eleven he moved to Indianapolis and married another woman, Josalie. My mom thought Josalie was a bitch, and my sister and I followed her lead. When I was thirteen, my dad asked my mom if my sister and I could spend the summer with him. It took some convincing, but my mom finally agreed to let us go.

I didn't trust many people, but I did still trust my mom at that time, so I went to Indianapolis thinking my dad was the asshole my mom said he was. After spending the summer with my dad, I found out it takes two to tango. My mom played her own part in their divorce, which only became apparent in hearing my dad's side of the story. After that, I no longer trusted my mom. I trusted nobody.

Living with my dad appealed to me because he had a more easygoing approach to parenting than my mom did: laxer rules and less nagging. Maybe he missed me, maybe he wanted me to love him, maybe he wanted me to fit in with the family, but he let me do almost anything I wanted to do.

My stepmom, Josalie, took care of her two kids, my sister, and me. She was sweet and loving. My mom wasn't the best cook, but Josalie made a delicious meal every night and packed us leftovers for lunch the next day. I had joined the swim team at the Jewish Community Center, which worked up my appetite, so I wholeheartedly appreciated that.

Eileen, one of my swim coaches, was a crazy, loud-mouthed, boisterous woman. "You can swim," she would proclaim authoritatively, "Everybody can swim." I found out by accident that I was good at the butterfly stroke. I'd always swam backstroke and freestyle, and I did okay. Then at one meet, someone was sick, and one of my other coaches said, "I need you to fill in for butterfly."

"I don't swim butterfly," I protested, "I mean, I do a couple laps of it in practice, but that's it. I don't know the turns."

"You're going to be in the outside lane," he said, "Even if you come in last, we still earn two points, and that's all we need. We just can't have the lane empty."

I swam it, and I won. My coach roared with laughter, "What was that?"

"I don't know," I said, even more bewildered than he was. Then I added quickly, "You didn't see that. I don't want to swim butterfly." But that was it. Every practice after that, he had me swimming butterfly.

My coach said, "You're good at this. This is what you're really amazing at." My swim coaches were wonderful, supportive, loving voices in my life. And, I was starving for that; I'd never received that type of encouragement from my family (at least it didn't seem like it at the time). Inspired by their encouragement, I started to coach a kids' swim team.

I also made friends in Indianapolis – I hadn't had many in New York. I met Scott, who was a straight lifeguard and hot as hell. I'd love to see what he looks like today. Scott would give me a ride in his red '68 Mustang, and we'd go out drinking together. *He's everything I want*, I'd swoon, *Can we get married?* Looking back, it was good that he was straight, because even if my intentions weren't pure, he was my friend and I needed to have that. At the end of the summer, I didn't want to leave. I finally had a family and friends.

Shortly before I was supposed to return to New York, I called my mom and told her I wanted to stay in Indianapolis. She was horrified.

"You're not staying there. No, that's ridiculous. School starts soon."

My summer had given me some much-needed confidence: "I don't want to live with you any more. I want to live with Dad. I miss him and you're a bitch." At the time I was telling the story to Jack, I had no awareness of how much I had hurt my mom. What must it have been like to have her son say that? I had no idea of how much I had hurt my sister either; it was her family that I wanted to walk away from too.

I lamented to Jack about how I begrudgingly flew back to New York, started eighth grade, and hated it. I never liked New York; I never fit in there and it never felt like home. There was always something mysteriously uncomfortable there, almost as if the house I grew up in was haunted. I couldn't stand it. And, I couldn't stand my mom's rules. She wouldn't let me go out, she wouldn't let me drink, she wouldn't let me do anything. And as a rule, when things got uncomfortable, I took action.

I had been doing my sister's paper route, my own paper route, mowing lawns, raking leaves, and I'd saved up a few hundred dollars. With that money I bought a one-way plane ticket from New York to Indianapolis. My mom didn't know I was leaving, and my dad didn't know I was coming.

I had a taxi pick me up two blocks from my house, timing it so I would leave in the window of time when my mom would be on her way home from work. Once my flight arrived in Indianapolis, I took a cab to my dad's house. It was dark out when I knocked on his door.

My stepmom opened the door and screamed.

I heard my dad call out, "Jo, what is it?" She closed the door.

I heard her muffled voice, "Uh, I think someone's here for you."

My dad opened the door and stared at me in disbelief, "What are you doing here?"

"I can't live with her any more. I can't do it," tears came to my eyes, "And I missed you. And I want to be here. I love Indianapolis. I love it here. And, I hate New York."

My dad and Jo looked at one another helplessly and let me in. After Jo fed me leftovers from dinner, my dad told me to call my mom. "She's probably worried about you."

"Where are you?" my mom snapped when she heard my voice.

"Indianapolis."

"What!" She exclaimed, bewildered.

"I'm with Dad and I want to stay here," I said.

There was a long silence, and then she said, "Have you discussed it with your father?"

"He told me to call you."

"Put him on the phone," she demanded. They talked for what seemed like hours, and finally agreed that I could stay.

I went to an amazing school in Indianapolis, North Central High School, and I joined the swim team. My dad diligently drove me to swim practice Monday through Friday at five in the morning.

Things were looking up for me. I even started to plan my future and set goals. I was going to go to Indiana University on a scholarship for their amazing swim program, and then I'd go to the Olympics. After my swimming career was over, I would be a sports commentator for the rest of my life.

Swimming then was a lot like yoga is for me now. It was a workout, it was stress-relieving, it was self-discovery, it was community. It was an alternative to getting drunk or doing drugs. But, just like yoga alone isn't enough to keep me clean and sober now, swimming wasn't enough to keep me out of trouble when I was a teen.

Every Night Has Its Dawn

In the version of my story I told Jack, my dad kicked me out because I was gay. Part of me wanted Jack to sympathize with me, but another part genuinely believed that was the truth. In any case, there was a lot more to the story than what I revealed.

As a teen in Indianapolis, you either spin donuts in your car during the snowy season or you drink. Or you do both. A friend and I used to drink peppermint schnapps in the mornings before school. We thought everyone would assume the mint smell on our breaths was gum. After school we'd drink Little Kings Cream Ales, which were only six or eight ounces and easy to chug. The members of the swim team drank like fish, so I was in good company. We would regularly throw wild keggers. I'd always wanted to host a party, mostly because people charged for the keg, and I thought, *What a great way to make some money.* When my dad and stepmom went away one weekend, I was finally able to do it, and it was amazing. I went to a school with 4000 people, so when word got out, tons of people showed up. My stepbrother and his friends were there, too. For me, having fun at a party was getting my friends wasted. That meant I could get drunk, too. My stepsister, who would disapprove of a non-chaperoned party, was getting home from work around one in the morning, so around eleven thirty we screamed, "Cops!" and everyone got out.

I had a guy from the swim team spending the night. My friend, my stepbrother, and I worked together to clean up every trace of the party, and then we went to sleep. We'd planned the perfect party. My dad and my stepmom would never know.

Then all of a sudden my stepsister was in my room screaming, "What the hell is going on here?"

"What are you talking about?" I grumbled, blinking the bleariness out of my eyes.

"What am I talking about?" she fumed, "Go downstairs. Just go downstairs."

I walked down the stairs and my step brother was there with at least ten people who had come back to continue to party. I couldn't believe it. "What the fuck, man?" I yelled.

He shrugged, "Some people came back over, and wanted to hang out for a bit, so I thought, like, whatever."

"What is wrong with you?" I shouted with unmasked exasperation.

My stepsister clued in, "You had a party. You had an effing party." I was busted. So much for the perfect party, my stepbrother sold me out. My stepsister wasn't about to cover for me – I used to steal her pot all the time anyway. I got in so much trouble, more love and attention, kind of.

My dad was already getting fed up with me because although I didn't have a driver's license, I did have a love of stealing cars. Specifically, my stepmom's Pinto automatic and my stepsister's stick shift – though it took me a while to figure out how to get the stick shift to start. For me, it was a high. I'd think, *Watch me get away with this*. I'd usually drive the car out to Holigay Park, a well known cruising spot where gay men could hide behind bushes to have sex or to just sit and drink. Some days I would spend hours there cruising around in circles.

My family didn't confront me right away, but I began to notice the spare car keys being hidden in ever more creative places. I took it as a challenge, and always found them. Finally, after my dad and stepmom came home from a week-long trip, they sat me down, and told me they'd written down the mileage on the car before they left and compared it to the mileage when they got home. There were 428 more miles on the car. My stepbrother had been out of town and my stepsister had her own car, so they knew it was me. "What gives?" my dad asked, "Where did you go?" I shrugged, "I don't know. Wasn't me." I thought, *Maybe I'm not the only one taking the car, that's a lot of miles.* All the cruising had added up.

It wasn't only cars that I stole. Once, I stole a beautiful blue opal and diamond ring from a guy I hooked up with. Part of my process now is to make amends, but I had no idea how to get in touch with him, so there was nothing I could do to repair that damage directly. Instead, I made a donation on an estimate of what I thought the ring was worth. I've since learned that sometimes the replacement value of things near and dear to the heart is priceless.

Later in life when I got to LA, I would break the law out of desperation, for survival; but when I was in Indianapolis, I was stealing just to steal. I felt empty, and I thought, *If I'm empty, you should be empty. If I don't have, you're not going to have. If I'm without, you need to feel what it's like to be without.*

When I got a fake ID, I started going to sex clubs. We had just moved into a new house in Indianapolis, and one night I gave my dad my usual excuse: "I'm spending the night at a friend's house." I was actually going to the bathhouse downtown. The bathhouse was in a sketchy neighborhood. I used to buy booze down there. The cashier was in a booth encased in bulletproof glass. You had to put your money into a rotating bin and they'd spin it around, take your money, put whatever you were buying in the bin, and spin it back out to you. It wasn't the safest area to walk around at night.

I loved the bathhouse. They had a shower, steam room, sauna, and rooms in the back. Upstairs was a lounge area, some more rooms, a big fabulous gym, and a disco dance floor where they'd blast new wave music and disco. They had a rooftop, and if it was warm out you could lay in the sun. They'd also have barbecues on Sundays. It was a place I could go where I could openly express a part of myself that I felt I had to hide everywhere else. It was my community.

That night it was slow, and I got bored. I left around three or four in the morning. *Now what?* I couldn't go back home, because I was supposed to be at my friend's house. I drove my scooter to our old house, which hadn't been sold yet.

I was no stranger to breaking into houses. A friend and I used to sneak out in the middle of the night to break into vacant properties – it was a high for me, I loved the thrill of being somewhere I wasn't supposed to be. The garage door was not locked, and I found the key for the door leading from the garage into the house in one of the regular hiding places. I parked my scooter in the garage, went into the living room, and fell asleep on the floor.

A few hours later, my eyes flicked open, as I heard the garage door click open. I rolled over and mumbled, "What the fuck was that?" I looked around. It was light out. *That was definitely the garage that just opened*, I thought.

"Leslie?" my dad called out.

"Yes?" I groaned. I got up and walked out towards the garage.

"What the hell are you doing here?"

"What are *you* doing here?" I retorted.

"I own this house," he threw up his hands.

"Well, things weren't great at Eric's. I had a hard time sleeping, and it was so late, I didn't want to bother you guys, so I just came over here to crash."

"Uh huh," he said, "Do I need to call Eric's parents right now?"

"For what? They're probably all still sleeping."

"I'm going to call to see if you were there or not. Do I need to make that phone call?"

"Um, no," I admitted.

"Where were you?"

I looked away.

"Why can't you tell me?"

We got in a huge fight. He kept trying to find out what I'd been up to and I kept refusing to divulge.

"Where were you?" he yelled at me, "We've got problems. We have got lots of problems."

"Well, maybe the problem is that I'm gay!" I screamed. That's how I came out to my dad. At the time that was an honest statement. I thought being gay was the problem. In Indianapolis, there were no healthy gay role models for me.

My dad searched my face as if thinking back over all the experiences he'd ever had with me, reconciling them with this new piece of information. Finally he mused, "Oh that's why you swim, to be around all those men."

"Oh my frickin' God." I yelled back, "You do know I get picked up every frickin' morning to practice from 5:30 a.m. to 7:30 a.m. before school. If you think I just want to be around men... Have you even ever tried to swim butterfly before? Then I practice two more hours after school. If you think I do all that just to be around men, you're insane." I continued, "I know where to see men with less than bikinis on – I don't need a swim team for that. I swim because I love to swim. It's a great escape. I can just let my thoughts go."

He went on to inform me we had some serious talking to do about rules and communication. All I could think of was all the maneuvering I was going to have to do to continue living the way I wanted to.

After this, we had many long discussions. He wanted me to go into therapy right away. I said, "I'm not going to therapy. I don't need to be fixed. It's okay that I'm gay. I'm actually really comfortable with it."

When my stepmom found out I was gay, she said, "I knew there was a reason you liked to go shopping with me."

"I don't know if that's a characteristic trait of gay people, shopping, but okay," I replied. I did love to shop, but that was beside the point.

"You should meet my hairdresser, Ken," Josalie bubbled, "My hair dresser's gay."

"No kidding," I said. I'd met her hairdresser before. Ken was a tall guy who was always in polyester bellbottoms, button down shirts that opened just enough to reveal his hairy chest, and big glasses. I continued, "Your hair dresser's a flamer. He's a can of Aqua Net," I said, referring to his Easter bonnet of streaky light gray-blonde hair that could go through a car wash without budging. He was the epitome of what people thought of as gay back then. I wanted to break the stereotype, but alas, I came to realize years later that I, too, am garden-variety.

The next time my stepmom got a haircut, I chatted with Ken, "So, fifteen, sixteen? And you already know?"

"Yeah," I said, "Didn't you know?"

"Yeah, I knew," he conceded. My stepmom laughed. She was cool with it, and we bonded during that period.

My stepsister didn't care either, "I knew it!" she said when she found out, "I just knew it." From then on she started asking my opinions on all her boyfriends.

My dad was the one who was uncomfortable with it. But, when he found out I was going down to the bathhouse in the bad part of town, he started driving me down there. He didn't want me going on my own. "Stay a couple hours, do whatever you need to do, and I'll pick you up," he would say. "Okay," I would reply, thinking, *This is awesome, I have a chauffeur.* My drinking accelerated, but it didn't strike me as a problem. I snuck into bars to meet other gay men, and that was just what we'd do. We'd get together, drink, and have sex. It was fun.

Two Lifestyles, One Lifetime

My drinking bothered my dad, though. My unapologetic attitude bothered him even more. He and I bowled in a Jewish men's bowling league on Sunday mornings, and if I went out drinking on Saturday night I would bowl great on Sunday morning. If I didn't go out drinking, I would bowl terribly. I presented this to my dad as evidence, concluding my argument with, "Daddy, drinking's good. Right?"

It got to be too much for him. One day he said, "You have to go back to New York. We're done with you. You're out-of-control and you don't want any help." I thought at the time that "help", meant they wanted me not to be gay. I didn't think he was talking about the drinking.

Years later when I made amends to my stepmom as part of my recovery process, she told me something I still don't remember: right before slamming the front door on them, I spat in her face. My immediate reaction was to laugh in disbelief, plus when I get really nervous and uncomfortable, I laugh; I couldn't possibly have hated myself enough to do that to another person. But, of course I knew she was telling the truth. This woman was forced to open her home to me, she cooked for me, and she cared for me – and when I left, I spat in her face.

To this day I cringe at the thought of the person I had become. Part of me still wants to deny it ever happened. But, glossing over my low points wouldn't do me or anyone else any good. This book is about recognizing our rock bottom behaviors and turning them into a strong foundation to help us return to loving ourselves and others.

Asteya

With some things I have stolen – cars, jewelry, money – I knew I was stealing when I did it. With other things, I didn't know I was stealing until after I'd done some work in yoga and recovery. Sometimes the amends I have to make are not because I was mean, crossed boundaries, or acted morally wrong; rather, it's that I've taken myself out of people's lives, stealing from them the experience of having a son, a brother, a friend. They say addiction is a family disease. It doesn't necessarily mean the other family members are also addicts. But, everyone in the family is affected by the addict's struggle in some way. People say, "The only person I really damaged was myself, because I took myself out of my family's life." Well, that had an effect on the family. I can see now that I followed in my dad's footsteps: disappearing and abandoning my loved ones. At the time I didn't see my leaving as abandonment. I looked at it as an escape, as taking care of myself. I didn't have any care or concern for those I left behind.

To make amends, I want to try to integrate myself back into people's lives, and it takes a lot of meditation to figure out what the next step is. Before I found recovery, I made decisions that destroyed some relationships beyond repair. Some people have chosen not to let me back into their lives. It saddens me because there's so much I'd like to share now that I'm sober and thriving. But there are people with whom, no matter what I do to mend the relationship, it will never be enough; they aren't able to let go of the pain I've caused them. Though I wish this weren't the case, it's not my job to spend a lifetime trying to convince them that I'm different now. After I make my amends, all I can do is wish upon them the same thing I do my yoga students: I hope they're leading a life filled with what they want to have and to experience. I also hope there are waves of great challenge, love, and frustration. It may seem strange to wish hardship upon my students and loved ones, but it's life's difficulties that force us to introspect, grow, and rise above. So, I pray for all to be guided during times of challenge and obstacles.

This is particularly important for those with addictions. Friends and family members who are codependent always show up to take care of the addict and clean up the mess. Don't do that. You may be interrupting someone's bottom. You might be stealing from them the exact thing they need to experience to find recovery. I wouldn't want them to miss that. On the one hand, we don't want them to go to jail or to the hospital, but maybe that is exactly what they need. Some people need something tragic to rock their world into reality. Through these experiences, people are able to step back and pause; to think, *What am I doing? Why am I doing it?*

When I first started teaching yoga, the practice of *asteya,* non-stealing, was still a challenge for me. I used to justify stealing things of little value, thinking, *With how much I do for the studio, they owe me a free coconut water.* In my head, I had earned what I took. After a couple of weeks helping myself to coconut water, the yogi in me would feel guilty and I'd put a twenty dollar bill in the cash drawer to make up for it, completely messing up the studio's cash balance accounting for the day. Even though I made amends, not stealing in the first place would have prevented the turbulence that others had to cope with.

The more refined my practice of *asteya*, the more subtle tendencies toward stealing I've identified in myself. A temptation for any yoga teacher is stealing people's time, running class late. Sometimes I have another fifteen minutes of stuff I'd love to give my students, but that too is stealing. When I run late, part of me wants to believe I'm like Robin Hood: robbing time spent working, stressing, driving, texting – maybe all at the same time – and giving time spent on spiritual practice. But that train of thought is masking selfishness and a need for control. It's more important that for the time I'm with my students, I give them my undivided love and attention, holding nothing back. The desire to steal arises from a sense of lack. Cultivating a sense of abundance comes partly from practicing *aparigraha*, non-greed, and partly from regulating relationships and activities that rob us of our energy.

Since I pour my heart into teaching, it's important that I keep my teaching schedule in check. If I'm teaching nonstop and expending all my energy on my students, that doesn't leave anything for my husband, Joe. As with any job, when things get busy, all that's left at the end of the of day is crumbs. It's lying, violating *satya*, when people ask if I'm available to do something, I say yes, and then I feel resentful about it. That's a sign that I need to reevaluate my definition of "available." When I keep my own energy from being completely drained, I am better able to practice *asteya* in my relationship with Joe.

PART III: APARIGRAHA

*Do you value what you have? How do you feel when someone
has something you do not? What is the result of comparing
others' external presentation of themselves to your own
internal experience of yourself?*

New York Minute

When I was on the plane back to New York from
Indianapolis, after I got kicked out, my dad apparently
called my mom and said, "He's on his way to New York.
He actually got on the plane. He has a drinking problem
and he's gay. Good luck." At the time, I didn't know my
mom had that information, and she didn't let on. But she
did try to draw it out of me.

For a couple of weeks I sat on my hands, but it wasn't
long before I was ready to get back to the lifestyle I'd
become accustomed to. When I started going out with
guys on the weekends, my mom began inquiring about
who I was going out with, how I'd met them, and what
we'd be doing.

One Friday night she was more determined for
answers than usual. When I told her I was going out
dancing, she wanted to know how I could get into a club

when I was underage. She reminded me that the house rules were different than at my dad's, and she didn't want to catch me drinking. I wove in as much truth as I could, telling her that there was a dance club I could get into and that I'd probably have a beer, but I assured her I wouldn't go overboard and I wouldn't drive (not that I had a driver's license yet anyway).

She tried a different approach, saying she wanted to meet the people I was going out with. She thought it was weird she hadn't met them yet. I started to get impatient and frustrated. She kept digging, pulling, poking, prodding.

"What's the name of the club?"

"I'm actually not sure where we're going tonight."

"What's the age range of the people who will be there?"

"Well, mostly twenties, maybe thirties."

"Is it going to be guys? Girls?"

"I think mostly guys, not too many women."

"Why not too many girls?"

Finally, I blurted out, "Well, I'm gay."

My mom began sobbing. She implored, "What have I done wrong? What does this mean? Are you going to be having sex?" My dad must have told her everything I'd been up to. "I've heard gay people are very promiscuous, and it seems like your behavior is along those same lines. Who are these people?"

"Well, there's Scott," I explained. "We're kind of dating."

"So you're already dating people!" she wailed, "You *are* promiscuous!"

The conversation went on and on like this. After all was said and done, I remember thinking, *I've hurt her. What I'm doing with my life is wrong. Being gay is bad.* Now I look back and think, especially since she already knew, she could have made that a much softer, kinder, more loving transition for both of us. However, just as I had no role models to show me how to be a healthy, balanced gay teen, my mom had no role models to show her how to be a parent to an unruly gay teen who's self-esteem had been plummeting for years.

Back to my old tricks, I regularly stole my stepdad's car to sneak out in the middle of the night. I'd go to bars, I'd go to sex spots – alleys and public bathrooms. We lived in a three-floor house, and I'd leave through the window in the bathroom on the basement floor. I knew my mom was a light sleeper, so I don't know how I thought I'd get away with it. One night I snuck out, and when I came back, the window was closed and locked. I went to the front door, but the chain was on. I quietly began to nudge it back and forth to get the chain loose. I finally got the door open, and my mom was standing right there inside the house. "Hi," she said, "You can go to sleep, but you are so grounded. We've got a lot to talk about tomorrow."

"Okay, I'll go to bed," I said, "And I'm not grounded, by the way. We'll talk about it. We'll definitely talk about it."

"This is my house, my rules." She raised her hand to me and said, "Don't let me catch you sneaking out again, or else."

I raised my hand back at her and said, "You don't or else."

"You wouldn't dare," her eyes narrowed.

"*You* wouldn't dare," I snapped, "I'm done being hit. I'm sixteen years old." We stared hard at each other menacingly, a snapshot of the heart-wrenching cycle that turns children who were punished with pain into adults who inflict pain. My mom gave up, lowered her hand, and never raised it to me again.

"This is my life. I'm out now," I stated.

"You're sixteen," she sighed, "And you're so promiscuous."

"What's wrong with that?" I said defiantly, "I don't care. I know who I am, I know what I want. I ran away from you. The only reason I'm back here is because dad booted me out. You don't want me here and I don't want to be here. We'll just deal with it." That didn't go over well with her. From that day on, I wasn't allowed in the house unless someone else was there.

A Hiccup Named Florida

As Jack cleaned up from dinner, I continued my story. He didn't ask too many specific questions, which was great. I told him how in New York I'd been hanging out with a guy named Charlie who liked to party the way I liked to party. His grandparents were moving to Florida, and they were buying two houses because, according to Charlie, they needed something to do with all their money. Charlie was going to go down to live in one of the houses, and he wanted me to come with him. He had been trying to get me to sleep with him for quite some time, but I wasn't that attracted to him. However, I needed to get out of New York.

I was working at Burger King at the time, and I started picking up double shifts and tons of overtime hours to save up money. After a few weeks of working like crazy, I told my mom I was leaving. This time, I didn't try to sneak out. I was upfront and told her I was going. And that was that. I dropped out of high school and left New York with Charlie.

Florida was a disaster. We were in the middle of nowhere: Port Richey and New Port Richey. Even with our combined ages, it seemed like Charlie and I were still fifty years younger than the next youngest person.

Charlie always wanted to have sex. I wasn't into it and I wasn't into him, but I did it anyway. I had no place to go and I didn't have a job; I needed a roof over my head and I needed food. I kept feeling worse about sleeping with someone I had become repulsed by, feeling worse about being stuck in that situation, and feeling worse about myself. What great training for a full career of prostitution.

About halfway through that summer, one of my cousins on my dad's side was in a car accident and died. He'd just turned twenty-one, and he and his friends had gone to Atlantic City for the evening. My cousin was not at all like me. He wasn't a drinker, a gambler, or a smoker, nothing. On their way back home that night, one of his friends fell asleep at the wheel and crashed the car into a tree. Nobody survived. It devastated the family. It devastated me.

At the funeral, I was a mess. I cried hysterically. One of my aunts came up to me. "Why are you crying?" she asked, "You barely had a relationship with him at all. What's your problem?" That hit me. I thought, *What's my problem? Which one? I have so many problems.*

My dad was there too. When he saw me, he walked over, "What are you doing here?"

I thought about Charlie's sweaty body against mine and shuddered. "I don't know," I mumbled, looking down.

After a few more weeks in Florida with Charlie, I couldn't handle it any longer. Being intimate with him felt gross now. I called my dad. "I don't know what I'm going to do," I told him, "I can't stay here anymore; I can't stand it. But I can't go back to New York. I can't deal with Mom."

"Well," he said slowly, "you can come back here, but there are going to be rules. One misstep and you're going to military school."

"Okay," I said, "I'll follow your rules."

"And you'll probably have to start junior year over again."

"That's okay too." I said. Every condition he gave me, I agreed to.

My dad and I agreed on a date that I would arrive in Indianapolis. I booked a ticket for three days before that date so I could spend some much-needed time playing with an old hook-up I was actually attracted to.

The day of my flight, I casually told Charlie I was going to the store to pick up a few things and that I was going to take the car. Charlie had a beat down car he had bought for about a hundred dollars that barely ever ran. I took a couple of things in a bag that I snuck into the car, but that was it. I left everything else behind. On my way to the airport, the car conked out on the Tampa Bay-St. Pete's Bridge, so I had to hitchhike a couple more miles to the airport. I never saw or spoke to Charlie again.

The day my dad thought I would be arriving in Indiana, I called him to tell him I'd make it to his house that afternoon.

"Do you want me to come pick you up at the airport?" he asked.

"No, it's okay," I said casually.

"When's your flight?"

"Well, actually I'm already in Indiana," I admitted.

"What do you mean you're already in Indiana?" he asked suspiciously.

"Yeah, I came a couple days early."

"So the whole idea that there are going to be rules doesn't apply for you?" he exploded.

"Well, starting today. That's what we agreed. Today," I rationalized, "I'm coming today, so that's when the rules start."

When I got to the house, my dad was pissed. The next day he drove me to a military boarding school, and they gave us a tour. He kept having side conversations with administrators, just out of earshot. On the way back, I asked, "What's the deal?"

"You said you were going to respect the rules," he shrugged, "Clearly you're not going to."

"I just got here," I protested. We argued back and forth for a while, before I realized, *This is fucked up, this is not going to work.* I sighed and asked resignedly, "When do I start?"

"Next week."

I'll pretend to be on my very best behavior, but I need to get out of here before I get sent to boarding school, I thought. And that's when I stole my dad's credit card, told the airline he was in a coma to get a flight booked, and ran away to Los Angeles.

Material Boy

After I'd told Jack my story, he looked at me thoughtfully and then asked me out of nowhere, "Can you put jam inside croissants?"

"What?"

"Can you serve coffee? Can you do anything like that? Because I have this friend, Ron, and he's looking for some help, and you need a job. You can't just sit in my house all day and do nothing. You need a job. And, we're not hiring you over at Jockster."

"But – ," I began. He was right though. Even after I convinced Carson, the guy who hired models, to sleep with me a few days later, he still wasn't willing to hire someone underage.

"I'm going to introduce you to my friend Ron tomorrow," Jack continued, "It's nothing fancy. Minimum wage. It's a little cafe called the Croissant Palace."

I looked down at my plate. "Okay," I said. It wasn't what I came to California for, but it was something. And I needed something.

"You know," said Jack, "you get to start your life all over again. And it can be whatever you want. If you want to do this modeling, fine. Have fun with it. Don't get caught up in all the craziness of it. Or," he continued, "you can get this job tomorrow, start slow, and build a brand new life for yourself."

I sighed sadly, thinking, *Here I am on my own, trying to do things my way, but there are still these walls I'm bumping up against. There are still people telling me "No."* However, in contrast to the other people in my life who had said, "No. Period." Jack was saying, "No, but here's another solution. Here's some help. Here's another way to go." Although I felt let down, I also felt taken care of. At the time, I knew Jack was taking care of me in terms of food, shelter, getting me a job, and connecting me with people. Looking back I see he also took care of me by not introducing me to anyone involved in pornography or prostitution (until I came back to him a couple years later). When we first met, he did everything he could to steer me away from that lifestyle.

The next day, I went down to the Biscuit Palace, as I would come to call it, to meet Jack's friend Ron. The Biscuit Palace was a little corner cafe that the owner had acquired, I heard in a good gossip session, through a five thousand dollar cocaine deal. Considering the circumstances, it turned out to be a rather successful business. It was across the street from a store called the Mayfair Market, which everyone called the Gayfair. The

Biscuit Palace had tall tables down the left side and display cases on the right side, and looked like it was perpetually waiting to be renovated – it had clearly been a while since its plain white walls had been repainted.

Ron managed the cafe by day to make ends meet, and was a musician and DJ by night. He was old-school gay; he didn't fit the West Hollywood mold. He had glasses and was one of the first guys I met with a handlebar mustache. I fell in love with him immediately. When he came out from behind the counter, I said to him, "This guy Jack, he said I should come here and talk to you."

"I know Jack," he said, sounding as if he'd hired a couple of guys like me before, "So, I suppose you come with no references except that Jack said to come see me."

"That's right," I confessed.

"Are you going to show up?" Ron asked.

"Yeah," I nodded.

"Are you going to steal all our food and eat all our profits?"

"No."

"And if we let you have breakfast here for free in the mornings, does that help you out?"

"Yes," I said emphatically. Ron gave me the job, and I ended up eating breakfast, lunch, and dinner there. I would make all sorts of to-go orders there to take home to stock my refrigerator.

When Ron found out I didn't yet have a place to live, he told me he'd introduce me to an actor friend of his who was looking for a roommate. Scribbling on the back of a receipt, he said, "This is going to be your pay check, and this is how much rent you're going to be able to give my friend, and the rest you can live on." Right away, I asked when the overtime shifts were so I could make more money. No matter how much my normal wage was, I still would've asked about working overtime. Whenever I got a taste of something I liked, in this case money, I wanted more, more, more.

I worked at the Biscuit Palace for a while. We would stuff a croissant with whatever you wanted. It turned out that asking coyly "What would you like me to stuff your croissant with?" was a surprisingly effective pickup line I could use on my male customers, and sensually preparing their order for them was great foreplay. Ron would often tell me to stop "over-serving" the customers. It was also fun working there because around the back there was a place called Texy Mexy. The food there wasn't great, but that's not why people went. Texy Mexy was known for their margaritas. It was packed to the gills from afternoon until closing. You could wait up to an hour and a half to get a seat sometimes. Some people would order standing up. The fire marshals used to come in all the time to reprimand the owners for letting too many people in. I would work all day at the Biscuit Palace then head over to Texy Mexy all night to get trashed. I met a lot of guys in both places.

Shortly after starting at the Biscuit Palace I desperately needed a haircut, and Ron suggested a "really cute guy" he knew named Bob who worked at a hair salon just a block away. I walked into the barber shop Ron recommended and saw a bald guy with a mustache. He had an amazing little body clad in a tank top and shorts that were shorter than anyone had business wearing. I thought, *That's got to be Bob. I'm in love.* "Cut. My. Hair." I said. We flirted the whole time. Afterward he said, "I'm going to go get a burger next door. Do you want to come along?"

"Yeah, definitely," I said.

As we sat there eating, he began the conversation, "So, what's your deal? Where did you come from?" Those conversations were always the same, I told people whatever they wanted to hear. I was good at watching people's reactions while I was talking. I made sure they found me interesting and agreeable so I could get more time with them. I was truthful in the sense that I told Bob

I was new to California and looking to build a life of my own. But I made stuff up about family and why I was running away.

I was a street, surfer-looking kid, which was totally his type. He was thirty-two, I was seventeen. *This is amazing,* I thought. Our fifteen-year age difference just added to the appeal.

"You probably don't need a haircut every day," Bob said, "but it would be great if you could swing by here on your lunch tomorrow." We were magnetized from the moment we set eyes on each other in the hair salon.

Bob had just graduated from a six-month recovery house program. He was busy going to meetings and was working a lot, so we were on and off. There were several men I was after, but Bob was my number one target. After a few weeks, we decided to move in together.

I thought to myself, *He's getting sober. I might have a little drinking problem, but this is going to work out just fine!* Though of course it didn't. Bob was new to sobriety. Looking back, I wonder what he was thinking. I know what I was thinking: *I need a place to stay, and here's this hot guy. I can do this for a while.*

Just as my parents had told my sister and I to keep the secret of their failed marriage while publicly playing out their drama in front of anyone who would be an audience, Bob was giving me mixed messages. He liked to get me drunk to live vicariously though me. Meanwhile, he was taking me to recovery program meetings with him because I had nothing else to do. This was the first time I had any experience with recovery programs. My dad had tried to get me into them in Indianapolis, but I resisted. As Bob and his group had their meeting, I'd clean ashtrays and coffee cups. The seed was being planted.

I also started going to support group meetings for friends and family of people in recovery. It was just something to do back then, but now I realize what an amazing resource these meetings are. Nowadays, people who are haggard from desperately trying to rescue loved ones from addiction or prostitution come to me for advice. Seeing that the person asking for help is exhausted, I prompt, "You're so focused on *them*. What have you done to get the support *you* need?" Often, we can't do anything to make someone change. They have to want it for themselves. Sometimes the only thing we can do is to get ourselves to a place where we are happy, healthy, and fulfilled. Maybe our example will be the thing that makes our friend or family member think, *I want that.* When they're ready to do the work, we'll have the energy and support network to give them direction and encouragement without falling back into codependence.

Tainted Love

I was brought up to think that you need to get an education so you can get a job, so you can make as much money as possible, so you can pay your bills, so you can have a comfortable death. I don't know if my parents were broke or if they were cheap, but my mom was always talking about money. I knew from a young age, *You have to have money.* As a kid I raked leaves, shoveled snow, mowed lawns, and did paper routes to make money. I used to comb the classified ads too. When I was nine, I said to my mom, "Mom, I'm going to apply for this job. What if I make more money than you? Would you be okay with that?" At nine years old I already knew to ask questions like that. I was already a corporate minded business guy, preoccupied with status and wealth.

Just as I'd scanned the classifieds as a kid, in LA my eyes were peeled for opportunities to get some more cash. To get from the actor's place out by the Hollywood Bowl to the Biscuit Palace, I had to bus through the area where guys were hanging out in the street prostituting. I thought to myself, *I could do that. I wonder how much money they make. I could totally do that.*

Bob lived above a dirty bookstore, Circus of Books. It was a sweet little studio apartment, but to me it was enormous. *Wow, our own space! How amazing is that,* I thought. I'd never known apartments before. I'd always lived in a house, so this was brand new, shiny, and exciting. Downstairs there was a ton of prostitution. After a few weeks of living there, while Bob was at work, I began working too – working the street in front of Circus of Books. I thought, *This is great, I don't have to commute that far for my job.* I started workin' from work too – sleeping with guys who came through the Biscuit Palace and Texy Mexy. This made Bob nuts.

"I know you're up to no good," he'd say to me as I was on my way out the door. "Who are you going out with?" I'd had this conversation many times before with my mom, so I was well practiced at it.

"Oh, just some friends," I'd say nonchalantly.

"From where? You don't have anywhere to go and meet people. You're too young to join a gym."

I'd shrug and hold back a smile, "I just meet them on the street."

"You're just meeting people on the street, becoming friends with them and just going out?" He'd looked at me skeptically, "Um, yeah right." Looking back, I realize he was a drug addict and an alcoholic in recovery. He knew the lying, the cheating, the thieving, and the bullshit. This conversation was familiar territory to him. I wasn't pulling anything over on anybody.

One night Bob said, "Don't go out tonight."

"Why not? I'm going out with my friend." I lied, "I'm helping him out, going shopping for some groceries. He broke his leg."

"You're going to sleep with him," Bob called my bluff.

"I'm just going to help him out," I insisted, trying not to smile, "I don't know about the other part."

"Listen, I'm not an idiot. The neighbors are telling me what you're up to, and I've heard from other people what you're up to. Don't go out tonight, you'll be sorry."

I rolled my eyes, "I'll see you later. I'm going out. I'm allowed to have friends."

When I got back home, the door was locked and the locks had been changed. The only thing I had ever learned to do in situations like this was to retaliate.

* * *

Right after my parents split, my mom still had some of my dad's credit cards and used them to take us on an extravagant vacation. We went to Florida first, then to San Diego. Then, we went to LA and did a tour of the stars' homes, which was actually a tour of the stars' fences. We also went to Universal Studios where I was picked out of a crowd of kids to be filmed for a green screen demonstration. When I saw my image up on the screen, I knew, *I'm going to be a star*. Then we went to San Francisco, we stayed at the Hyatt downtown, where my sister and I spent a whole afternoon going up and down the glass elevators. Thirty-six years later I taught at the Yoga Journal Conference in the same hotel we stayed at back in 1977. San Francisco was supposed to be our last stop, but when we were getting lunch in Chinatown, we met a couple who told my mom about Las Vegas, "There's this place called Circus Circus. You can take your kids. They can play games. You're out here anyway, you should go."

"Yeah, okay. I'll just extend the trip," my mom smiled wryly. "I don't care, I'm not paying for it."

When we got home from the trip, my mom's car was gone. My dad had it towed while we were on vacation. That's how the divorce was. If she did something, he would do something back to her. Looking back now, I know much of the anger my parents unloaded on my sister and me was misdirected. They were playing out their marriage problems on us. I know that, because I know how I've acted out in my own relationships. At times I've been violent, and it had nothing to do with the other person. It had everything to do with my own rage and my own upset at who I am as a person. How I reacted to Bob changing the locks is one example.

* * *

I'd been stashing money from all the hustling under a floorboard in Bob's apartment. I had about a thousand bucks, which back then seemed like a million dollars. I tried to get in. I kept pounding on the door and yelling, but no one answered. *I'm really going to have to bust this door down*, I thought. It didn't dawn on me that at some point Bob would come home, he'd open the door, and I'll be able to get my stuff.

I knocked on one of the neighbors' doors, still red in the face, and asked, "Do you have a hammer or screwdriver to help me out with something?" He looked at me cynically, and shut the door before I could protest. Something switched in my head. I clenched my fists and marched back to Bob's door. Driven by adrenaline, I took in a big breath, and then threw my weight against the door, busting it down. Sweaty and drunk on rage, I stumbled into the apartment. I must have had some kind of psychotic split. I can't say it was a blackout, because I remember everything I did: I destroyed the apartment. I destroyed everything that was important to him. I slashed the tires on his new bicycle. I killed some of the fish in the amazing saltwater tank he had. Bob had baked a big chocolate cake, and it was sitting on the table. It didn't say, "Happy Birthday, Les," that's for sure. A couple weeks earlier he'd painted the whole apartment white. In a rage, I dug my hand into the cake and began smearing it everywhere. Everything that was white, I made it chocolate cake-colored: walls, ceilings, everything. I destroyed the place. Then I got my money and left. *Nobody breaks up with me*, I thought, self-righteously, *I do the breaking up.* The movie *Pretty Woman* hadn't come out yet, but when it did, I would adopt one of Julia Roberts' lines as my personal tag line: "I say who, I say when, I say how much." I needed to be in control.

Bob's sponsor had a sponsor, and after trashing the apartment, I went to his place to spend the night. His name was Frank and he lived with his sister Aura. I kept calling Bob and left numerous messages on his answering machine: "Pick up." "I know you're there." "Bob! Pick up." He wouldn't pick up his phone. I found out later that he was staying with a friend who *he* was sleeping with. At that time in my life, I didn't always have a sense that I was creating big messes in the moment, but I always had a sense of urgency to clean the mess up once it was created. Bob was doing something that was separating us and that freaked me out. He was saying, "No," and I don't do no.

Watcha Gonna Do When They Come For You?

The next day I was at the Biscuit Palace working and in walked two cops. *That's hot*, I thought. They casually asked me questions about the food: "Which croissant is this?" "What's this flavor?" And then the kicker: "Is your name Les Leventhal?"

"Yes," I said calmly.

"Would you come over here and talk to us for a minute?"

"Sure, okay," I walked coolly out from behind the counter.

"Could you turn around and put your hands on the wall." It was more of a statement than a question.

Oh my God, I'm being arrested. I turned around slowly and hung my head to rest my forehead on the wall.

They took my wrists, cuffed my hands behind my back, and read me my rights.

The police officers took me to the West Hollywood prison tank on Santa Monica Boulevard, right in the center of town. Walk a few blocks in either direction, and there's a ton of nightlife and it's bustling with people, but around those concrete government buildings it's a dead zone. Everything inside was metal and cold, and the lights were super bright. It seemed like there was no one around in the whole jail, it was just me. I was there for hours. Then, after it got dark, someone finally showed up and unlocked my cell. They shipped me up to Sylmar Juvenile Hall. When I got booked in, the guy said, "Well, this is your home for a while." I thought, *I'm in jail. What the fuck?*

I was allowed one phone call, so of course I called Bob. When he picked up, I blurted out, "Can you get me outta here? I love you. How could you do this to me? I'm sorry, I won't do it again, I'm so sorry, please come help me." Bob said flatly, "You're a fucked up mess and you need a lot of help. Don't call back," and then hung up on me.

Boy did I get teased in juvie. One of the guards jeered, "What's wrong with you? A nice Jewish boy from New York – ain't Mama got a fancy attorney to spring you out of here?" That night, I lay in the cell I was sharing with another guy and cried all night long. I felt stupid, and I was scared. I had no understanding of what was going on. I knew what I did, but I didn't know it was wrong. I tried to figure out what I did to get caught. Or what didn't I do that would have prevented me from getting caught. I thought, *I'm not a criminal, I'm just in love.*

I didn't know what was going to happen. I didn't know if I'd be in there for days or for the rest of my life. No one was telling me anything about what was happening on the outside. By the second day they had me taking math and science classes in there. *This is ridiculous*, I thought, *I can't believe I'm in here*. That night I was too cold to sleep, and I spent all night crying again. After three or four days of this, I was exhausted. Then, while I was slumped in a chair in one of my morning classes, the door opened. "Leventhal?" a voice boomed.

"Yeah?" I responded.

"Come with us."

I followed the men to an office, where they sat me down and one of them asked me, "Are you willing to leave the state?"

"What?"

"We've talked to Bob, and he's willing to drop the charges, but you have to agree to a few conditions. You have to leave the state. There's a plane ticket from LA back to New York, and if you're willing to get on the plane, you're out of here."

"Who bought the ticket?" I asked, bewildered.

"Your mother." My whole body stiffened. When I didn't say anything, he continued, "We have to send you back to your mother because you're under eighteen." I crossed my arms and sat back in my chair. *The police are going to take me back to that house*, I thought, barely able to believe it. *Just like when I was seven*. Sensing my resistance to go back to my mother, he continued, "Your alternative is to stay in here."

"For how long?" I asked, of course, weighing my options.

"I don't know the answer to that question."

I considered that for a few more moments, and then decided, "I need to get out of here."

They drove me to the airport in handcuffs, and took me through the airport in handcuffs. They walked me to the plane, onto the plane, and into my seat. They put my seat belt on. Then, they finally uncuffed me. They told the flight attendants, right in front of me, "He needs to be watched." I looked down at my feet and my cheeks burned.

Once the plane got off the ground, one of the flight attendants came up to me and said, "There aren't going to be any problems here, are there?" I started crying. She smiled kindly and said, "Okay, good. You're going to be just fine."

Sensing her sympathy, I asked, "Can I have a drink? A Southern Comfort Manhattan?" Just because incomprehensible demoralization had just walked by me in the form of 200 other passengers, doesn't mean I didn't have a little *chutzpah* left to try to numb out for a bit.

"No," she said bluntly, and continued down the aisle shaking her head.

I got to New York, and my mom was waiting for me at the airport with my stepdad. It wasn't a very affectionate hug hello. In the car, we were all quiet. In my head, I mulled over the certainty that I'd be forced to go back to school in New York. *Ugh,* I thought, *But, at least now the kids will accept me, I've been to juvenile hall. I'll really fit in.* My mom broke my train of thought when she looked at me in the rear view mirror and said coldly, "So, what's your plan?"

"For what?"

"Here's the deal. You left here a few months ago. You chose to leave. And, I'm really happy with you being gone. You can stay here for a week – seven days – but you're not allowed in the house if no one else is there. This isn't a one-way ticket, it's a round trip to wherever you want. You can go anywhere, but you're not staying here."

For a moment I was stunned. *You bitch,* I thought. Then the shame and humiliation set in. We'd been having an ongoing battle for years, and I felt as if she had won. *Damn I didn't see that one coming,* I thought, *Checkmate.* Aloud, I replied, "Okay, whatever." A week later, I was right back in Los Angeles.

Open-Bar Mitzvah

When I got back to LA from New York, I went back to Frank and Aura's place to sleep on the couch. I ended up staying with them for quite a while. I called Bob right away, "Hi-i! I'm back."

"I knew you were back today," he beamed, "I felt something, that you were back."

Just like that, as if nothing had happened, we were back to our on-and-off relationship. That's the funny thing with drug addicts, alcoholics, relationships and love – even though both of us must have known it wasn't right, we couldn't resist it. Not only that, a seed of drama was planted in my genes, and my childhood experiences fertilized it, nurtured it, and had an irrigation system installed.

* * *

When I had my *Bar Mitzvah* back when I was thirteen, neither of my parents had yet signed their divorce papers. Looking out at the audience from where I stood, in the front row to my left, was my dad and my stepmom-to-be, who had come from Indianapolis to be there. On the opposite side were my sister and my mom, who was, of course, livid that my dad had brought his girlfriend. In the back row, as if no one would notice, was my stepdad-to-be and his kids.

The celebration for my Bar Mitzvah party was a stark contrast to the *Bat Mitzvah* my sister had shortly before my parents separated. Her's was at the lavish Huntington Town House, a fairytale ball venue, and was attended by a couple hundred friends and family members from both my parents' sides. Everyone seemed so happy, and all those guests meant she got a haul of money and savings bonds. My Bar Mitzvah was less about people coming together and more about people torn apart. After the ceremony, my mom drove us an hour and a half back out to Long Island for a modest party with her side of the family. Then in the evening, I went to a dinner my dad arranged at a small place out in Brooklyn with twenty or thirty members of his side of the family. My friends, Matt and Doug, who got to go to both parties, thought having two parties was the coolest thing in the whole world. I was mortified. It was supposed to be a happy day, but all I could do was pretend. At the end of the night, I counted up all the money and it was less than my sister had received. I was jealous and pissed. *I should get the same or more than my sister got,* I thought, *She got the best years of their marriage, I deserve something to make up for that.*

Years after my Bar Mitzvah, I found out that more had gone on that day than I'd realized. My dad had a flair for the dramatic, which I inherited from him, and at my Bar Mitzvah ceremony, he pulled my mom aside and said, "I know we all have lives going on, but if you take me back I'll drop everything and change for you." When I heard this story as an adult, I thought, *Oh my God. I've done that before.* To men. To Bob. It never works. Not for long, anyway.

* * *

One night, after lots more on and off with Bob, I got a call from a hotel called Crystal Sandy Hotel, which was affectionately known as The Fisting Palace. It was a hotel where you could check in (or sneak in) to do drugs or do men – no questions asked. I liked to check in and do drugs for days; it was the real Hotel California.

"Hello?" I answered the phone.

"Hi, I'm calling from Crystal Sandy Hotel. Is this Les Leventhal?"

"Yeah," I said, feeling for my wallet. I thought I must have forgotten something there.

"Do you know Bob Creal?" the man asked with forced calmness.

"Yes," I replied hesitantly.

"There's a piece of paper inside his wallet that says in an emergency to call you."

I paused, "Okay."

"We need you to come down here."

When the manager let me into the room, there was Bob, sprawled out on the bed unconscious. Looking at the dresser, it was as if I'd walked into a bar. He must have been having the most amazing party. I'd never seen so much booze in my life. And there were needles everywhere. Maybe that image is what prevented me from ever shooting up. Here was this guy who I tried to manipulate into taking care of me, and he was completely helpless and hopeless. I felt heavy as I imagined his open door at night and the many men who surely came in and out of his room for sex. That was a carelessness that I, too, would soon welcome into my life, and it would eventually cripple my soul.

In a tone that indicated this was a regular inconvenience, the manager said, "Can you get him home?" They gave me one hour to wake him up and get him out of there, and they insisted that I didn't call the police. This was the first time I'd had to help anyone in serious trouble. After about forty minutes, he regained just enough consciousness to say some rather unpleasant things about seeing me in the middle of his "fun." I called some of his recovery brothers and we were able to get him back to his apartment – the same place I'd destroyed a couple years earlier. His friends had an intimate understanding of relapse – an understanding I would also have a close-and-personal relationship with in the years to come – and, they took him to a detox.

Once Bob was back home after detox, we got together and he sat me down at the table. "This thing we do, you and me, I can't do it any more," he said.

"Me either," I agreed.

Bob has since passed away from a deadly overdose due to a disease that shows no mercy to anyone that thinks time is the healer. To this day, he is still one of my greatest teachers. My experience with relapse years later, long after Bob died, helped me understand his self-destructive choices. I relapsed because I wasn't doing the work required to stay in recovery. I was doing the same thing over and over again expecting different results, which I now understand is insanity. I tried so hard to make my relationships fix my emotions and my low self-esteem. I was not able to comprehend the disease concept that when I put substances of any kind into my body, my craving for more awakens (I can still experience this today with coffee and sugar – oh and yoga). With my own experience of relapse and the struggle through shame, guilt, and feelings of being a failure again, I have been able to cultivate a real sense of *karuna*, compassion, in my own life and for the lives of others, especially when people close to me relapse.

You Can't Always Get What You Want... But You Can Sure Try

Shortly after getting back to LA from New York, I got a receptionist job at Acura in Santa Monica. This was when Acuras first came out. I was still casually prostituting at night, but I wanted to make as much money as possible during the day, too. I went in for the interview wearing casual slacks and a short sleeve plaid shirt that definitely didn't say dress shirt. A Jewish guy from New York interviewed me.

I took a deep breath, looked him straight in the eye, and said, "I don't know what this job is exactly, but it sounds like it's easy. Like, I just have to answer the phone and greet customers, and do follow up calls. I haven't worked as a receptionist before, but I know how to figure stuff out and I'm great with people. I'll do anything to get this job."

He looked me up and down, "Are these the best clothes you have? Did you wear your best clothes to this interview?"

"Yes."

"If we give you money will you go buy two pairs of pants and a couple shirts?"

"Yes. Definitely."

They gave me the position, and I kept it for about six months. I drank a lot on the job. I used to take the bus there from Frank and Aura's, where I was still staying, in West Hollywood. There was a little deli on the corner where I caught the bus, and I would stop off there and get little half-cans of piña coladas and daiquiris so I could chug a couple on my way to work. Now that I was liberated from Bob and no longer around the recovery community all the time, I was physically and mentally free to drink a little more. A little older and wiser than when I'd first arrived in LA, it was also easier for me to get into bars.

I'd been staying with Frank and Aura for a while, and I needed a break from them. I wanted to get away for the weekend, and I'd always heard about Palm Springs; that's where the stars went to vacation. So I bought myself a bus ticket and took the three and a half hour bus ride down there. I stayed at the Desert Bunk-In Boarding House, which I'd found through a gay guidebook. It was a house for people without food, shelter, or jobs. Back then, I stayed there because it was cheap, but looking back, I know that the money I paid to stay there helped them. On the first night, there was a dinner in the house, and they invited me to come in as a guest. It had been a long time since I'd been invited anywhere.

The next afternoon, I found a bar, and this guy walked in, Michael. We were wearing the same outfit: white tennis shoes, tight blue jeans, and a button down shirt with big thick blue stripes, thin white stripes in between them, and a white collar. I was in love by the end of the hour, and it was on for the rest of the weekend. When we went back to his place, I met his sister and his other hilarious roommate. We had fun talking and joking. I still smile thinking back to that weekend. Michael and I played the whole next day until I had to get on my bus back to LA.

He came up to LA the following week and we played some more. Michael and I continued to travel back and forth between cities, and we ran wild. He treated me great, and I couldn't get enough of him. Eventually he moved to Washington, DC, and it was like going through withdrawal for me; I wanted more. My longing was so intense, that I even went to visit him there once.

"What are you doing in DC?" he asked, "Work stuff?"

"I came here to see you," I said, smiling.

"Oh," he said hesitantly, "that's a long way to come just for a fuck." I was speechless. Obviously the unquenchable desire I'd been feeling wasn't mutual. That was the last time I saw him.

Despite all the partying, I kept managing to show up for work. After a while, I realized I wanted something more than the job I had at Acura, and I wanted to make more money, so I applied for a job at a computer company. The interviewer said, "You really don't have enough skills, but you seem to have the chutzpah to learn quickly. And you're from the East Coast, so I know you're not going to be like these LA boys, trying to go surf or play and party." I couldn't hold back my laughter.

I worked my butt off at that job though. And then I got another job at the Executive Compensation Consulting Group. It was hoity-toity, especially for back in the eighties. Between this job and prostitution, I was making good money. Things were looking up. I had started a new life for myself, just like Jack had said I could do on that second night I spent in LA.

Then, one day, one of my bosses called me into his lavish office. He said, "So, all this overtime. You know, we didn't hire you to pay you this much."

I was taken aback, "Well then stop giving me all this work. This is more than one person's work. I can't do it any faster. I already type at eighty-five words a minute, and that's faster than anyone else here."

I nodded compliantly as my boss went on to list off all the things the company needed me to be, and all the rules they needed me to follow, which were definitely not Les' set of rules. "Yeah, okay," I nodded, thinking, *This guy doesn't know what he's talking about*, "Yup, got it," *What an asshole*, "Yes, sir," *What a schmuck*. I had no ability to understand, respect, or conceptualize why other people had rules. I didn't see how what anyone else wanted should affect my life unless they had drugs, alcohol, money, or tickets to some event. Or they were hot.

I walked back to my desk, calm and collected on the outside, fuming on the inside. I sat there for a bit staring at my computer screen without processing what I was seeing. My rage mounted, until finally I pushed the mouse aside and stood up. *Asshole,* I thought.

I stormed back into my boss's office.

He raised an eyebrow, "Yes?"

"I thought about what you said you wanted, and I think you're fucked up, I quit. Now." I slammed my keys down on the desk and marched out. The thought that came into my mind had crossed it many times before, when parents, teachers, or even lawmakers had tried to enforce boundaries: *Your rules don't apply to me.*

Aparigraha

Aparigraha, non-coveting, non-greed, is one of the *yamas* in yoga. It's work for me. As far back as I can remember, I've been preoccupied with money and I've been haunted by a deep-seated jealousy for anyone who had something more than me, or even just something different. Even today, I still catch myself coveting other yoga teachers' student bases, support networks, or notoriety. You can't have it all, but I try. It's as if there's a little kid in me who taunts, *Watch me get away with this. I can figure out a way to have everything I want.* When I experience something that feels good, my first thought comes from the addict in me: *More, more, more.*

The wonderful, beautiful thing about practicing yoga in a group class is that it gives us an opportunity to experience jealousy, greed, and desire, and to practice calming those flames, rather than letting them consume us. It's a chance to practice cultivating happiness for others' gifts. When I first started yoga, I was an aggressive weightlifter and I was used to heaving and grunting through my exercises. I was in a hot sweaty class with Rusty Wells, one of my first teachers, and he gave us the option to go into *hanumanasana*, full splits. As I was wrenching my body into a contorted version of the pose, Rusty said to the whole class, "Do you think the people in full splits are happier than those of you who aren't?" I thought, *Definitely, yes, absolutely,* and pushed even harder against the resistance of my muscles. Rusty calmly walked over to my mat, and with the joy and sing-song that always hangs in his voice, he said to me,

"This pose is dedicated to the lord *Hanuman*. Show some respect. For now, take *ardha hanuman*, half splits." So I did. In the less intense version of the pose, I could actually breathe. Instead of contracting to protect my body, my bulky muscles began to stretch and lengthen. In that moment, I realized I didn't have to have it all at once. It was okay that there was still work to do. It was okay to be in half splits. Some days it's okay to just be grateful to have a life at all and a body that can practice yoga.

Yoga is not about improving the body, it's about accepting it. Especially when I was a weightlifter, thirty pounds heavier, I used to think miserably, *I'm fat, bald, and hairy from the neck down*. After many years of practice, now I no longer think of myself as fat, but I am bald and hairy from the neck down, and that's okay. I still have bumps in the road, but now I don't have the daily struggle with self-esteem that went on for years. That's so important, because in the blink of an eye, "Nobody likes me. Poor me" can turn into "poor me – pour me a drink." Yoga has let me recognize how great it is that there's no one else like me. It has allowed me to be the best me I can be, instead of trying to copy someone else. Instead of trying to have what I want, it's a daily practice for me to want what I have. Once I could grow the muscles of respect, patience and tolerance, and learn to ease into a pose, relax at the edge, and not try to push, thrust, or jam through it – that's when my whole practice transformed. That's when full splits started to show up for me.

In my yoga classes, I say to students, "The experience you're having inside your body right now – do you want that? Are you grateful for that? So, you've got tight hamstrings; can you be grateful that you have hamstrings at all? Grateful that you have legs? Grateful that you even have a body?" When I have students sitting in watch-*asana* or standing HOH pose (hands-on-hips), I say, "When you see people around the room are taking challenging variations, can you look at that person and think, *Thank you*. Thank you for expressing yourself. Thank you for showing me something beautiful." Sometimes that's how we experience poses, by watching, not by doing. That's still yoga.

When we practice *aparigraha* on the mat, this habit will persist off the mat. I used to think, I'd be happy when I got away from my parents, I'd be happy when I got to California, I'd be happy when I got the job, got the boyfriend, got the promotion. When I started yoga, it was the same: I'll be happy when I get into full splits, when I get my foot behind my head, when I do a one-arm-handstand. But, the habit of thinking, *I'll be happy when...,* guarantees that these achievements will never make us happy. The moment we get them, we'll find something else to covet. How could it be any other way if we only ever practice being in a state of greed and jealousy? Once I started practicing *aparigraha* in yoga, the way I perceived my life started to change. Now, I am overcome with how much I have been gifted in this life.

Several years ago, I took a workshop at the Yoga Journal Conference with Aadil Palkhivala, a jolly, bald master teacher from Seattle. He sat in *baddha konasana*, a seated pose with the soles of the feet touching, and he opened up his feet so wide that the tops of his feet, including his big toes, touched the floor. He said, "Do you think I'm happier because I can do this and it seems like everybody else cannot?" He looked at all of us and waited, and we all just smiled back at him shyly. Finally he beamed, "Here's the answer: I am. Most certainly." We laughed at his unexpected proclamation. He went on to clarify that although doing *baddha konasana* brought him joy, it didn't mean he was better than us.

We all have a different purpose, or, as I frequently remind my students, "We all have different gifts and challenges." This reminds those experiencing joy and those who are suffering that they are no different from each other. No one deserves more than another. In poses with tons of variations for students to take, I coax people to connect with their own purpose, "Maybe you're being offered a gift right now, but you're missing out on it because you're caught up and struggling to grasp at somebody else's gift." When it comes time to leave a pose I encourage the students who are in bliss to practice *aparigraha*: "Let go of your gift without holding on or grasping so that others have a chance to experience theirs."

Experiencing, dancing with, and overcoming greed on the yoga mat has helped me redefine my relationship with money. I do want to make money in my life, but I want to make just enough to support a fulfilling life. I hope to have a low enough income that I can't do everything I want to do. It's important to have gifts and challenges on and off the mat.

In the Yoga Sutras, Patanjali says that the yogi who is established in non-possessiveness will come to understand the how and why of existence. When we move away from greed, transition from selfishness to selflessness, we start to take care of each other. Sometimes, I think all the natural disasters we've been having in the world lately are Mother Nature, or God, or the Universe urging us to help each other. Maybe one day there will be enough damage that we'll have to revert to the way people live in Bali: in compounds with families. In Bali, if members from one compound go next door in need of help, the other compound opens its coffers or reaches into the bank to pull out money, and they help. There's no question of how long you've been at your job, your income level, or your credit score. In America, if you let lenders know you're in dire need – you have no money, your child desperately needs healthcare – they take it as a cue to ramp up your interest rate because they know you're in no position to negotiate.

To find balance, I have to make sure I'm not taking more than I'm giving back. That's part of what teaching yoga is about for me. Because of all the experiences afforded me, I have been able to foster gratitude and awareness, and I feel it's my duty to share that with others. I'm a selfish guy, and I want to keep it all for myself, but I understand that I can't keep things unless I give them away. In my experience, when I've let go of the gifts I've received, it's made space in my life for even greater gifts than I could have ever imagined and I have a wild imagination.

PART IV: ISVARA PRANIDHANA

What are you devoted to? What can you surrender to? What makes you feel supported? Which practices give you a sense of unity and oneness with your community or with the world at large?

Could You Take My Picture? 'Cause I Won't Remember

When I was eighteen in California, I got my driver's license. I was finally old enough to join a gym. Wanting to fit in in LA, getting my body in shape was of paramount importance. The hot men I was meeting at the gym were also of paramount importance. I was constantly trying to see if I could sleep with the right person to break into movies – porn or Hollywood, whichever one was going to get me famous.

I was working at a geological consulting firm in Long Beach, and the commute was crazy, so eventually I moved into a tiny apartment in Long Beach. It was about $400 per month, and I was making about $1,000 a month after taxes. Monday to Friday was for work, and my weekends were for drinking. Friday night would always start in the same way: I would get a bottle of Korbel champagne, which was expensive. Spending fifteen or twenty dollars on champagne was huge for me. Then, I would get take-out from King Sushi, and I would eat and drink all of that alone, celebrating the freedom of living by myself.

By the time I was nineteen, my body was in amazing shape. I looked at myself in the mirror, and thought, *Now I'm ready for modeling.* I didn't get into porn out of a place of desperation or need. It was from a conscious, aware place.

I went back to Jockster Magazine, and this time they booked a photo shoot with me, immediately.

At the end of my first shoot, I said, "Wow, that was really interesting."

"You know," said the director, "if you want to do more, I can definitely get you connected to the right people. I'm actually doing something with another company for a movie soon, and I can bring you in for a scene or two."

I didn't think twice about the repercussions of the career path and lifestyle I was diving into. "Sure, sounds great," I exclaimed.

In Long Beach, I moved into a house in Belmont Heights. My roommate, Mikey and I lived downstairs, and these great lesbians, Brenda and Debbie, lived upstairs. Brenda was a probation officer. Not mine. She was bisexual, and it felt like sometimes she was trying to get me to sleep with her. All four of us used to go out to the beach all the time, work on our tans, smoke a lot of pot, dabble in some other drugs – cocaine and speed. I'd always done a little bit of everything, but now I'd started seeking out how to purchase stuff myself.

Brenda, Debbie, and Mikey were my family. Brenda was motherly and Debbie was uncannily fatherly. They yelled and screamed at each other when they fought, just like my parents. For a while Mikey felt like a brother. We'd all go upstairs or downstairs. We all used to attend the Church of Religious Science together. Then, on Sunday afternoons, our house was party central. We'd have people from church over for barbecues every weekend. I was spending time with family, friends, and people who were fun to be around. Before things got way out of control, it was almost healing. It was amazing.

I kept attending this church for several years. I even called my mom and said, "I'm not Jewish any more." She cried, just like she cried when I came out to her. I loved freaking her out.

When I go to churches and temples, I don't hear the religion. I hear the message of love, community, and healing. It's been like that my whole life. I have compassion for people who take away the message *I'm a bad person, I'm leading a bad life, and I'm going to be damned to hell.* I don't know what that's like, not from those gathering, worshipping places.

I remember the first time I walked in. The church was in an outdoor mall in Huntington Beach. It was very LA, chic and cool. I thought, *I can fit in here.* Reverend Peggy was standing up front. She was super tall and always had amazing gowns that would show through these beautiful silk robes she wore. And, she had gorgeous scarves. I found out later she had Lou Gehrig's disease. She was a powerful woman with a powerful message about leading a full, purposeful life. During the sermons I would always cry, because I felt connected there. I'd think, *I understand life. I have meaning. I have purpose.* I used to do classes there, six- or eight-week series. I was even tithing, parting with some of my money.

I loved that place. It relieved me of isolation. I had friends, family, love, and I didn't have to sleep with anyone to get it. I didn't have to take my clothes off. I didn't have to tell crazy-ass stories for people to want to hang out with me. People knew what I was doing for a living, but no one ever judged me. I finally felt a sense of belonging.

At the time, I thought, *This is great. I have balance in my life. On the one hand I'm prostituting and doing all this other crazy stuff, but at the same time I have friends. I have a family.* It wasn't dark yet. It was still fun.

The Church of Religious Science was my last unconscious attempt to find myself, to do something with my life before my life spun out of control. And, it just didn't work. That said, it planted seeds in me. Underneath the insanity of everything I was doing, it helped shape an ideal and a thin thread of morals, even though I was out breaking the law and hurting people. To me, I wasn't intentionally trying to be bad, I was doing what I needed to do to thrive.

Eat, Sleep, Play And Get Paid For It

In 1989, pornography and prostitution took off for me. Although I was prostituting on-and-off before that, I could start charging more when I got a name for myself in the porn industry. I began getting invitations to perform in strip clubs, dance clubs, and bars all around the country. With that comes more hustling. The gigs paid okay, but the real money was in the people there asking, "Do you want to come spend an hour with me?" The answer was always, "Um, yeah." A visiting prostitute can charge much more. That's when I started making big bucks. And, with all that came free booze and free lines of lots of things.

The larger sums of money meant I didn't have to do the odd secretarial job any more, and this let me go crazy. Crazy with sex, crazy with alcohol, crazy with drugs. Brenda, my roommate, said to me one day, "You need a mantra if you're going to do this." She thought for a moment, "Eat, sleep, play and get paid for it." *Eat, sleep, play and get paid for it*. I loved that. So that's what I did. For a while I thought it was so fun. I used to say to myself, *This is amazing. I get to do all this stuff, sleep with hot guys for the movie parts, stay in amazing places. Then, when it's over I get paid and I get to go do whatever I want.* That felt wonderful.

I did both print work and movies, sometimes with condoms, sometimes without. Everyone kept asking if I'd done anything yet; they wanted to hire someone new. A fresh name, a new face, an unexplored body. The industry is all about who's the next new gonna-be-something-hot. I played off the idea that there was no one out there being The Jew in the industry. I thought, *This has got to be something*. Porn movie producers kept on asking me if I'd done any work yet. Most of what I'd done was still in production, so I kept saying, "no," "no," "no," "no," "no." But all of a sudden everything exploded out on the shelves. Some of my friends reacted with disgust: "Oh my God, I can't believe you're doing this," but others raved: "Oh my God, so great. How fun. I wish I had the guts to do that."

With the work I was doing, I fell into a circle of, I hesitate to say, friends, but they were the people I was hanging out with at the time. We spent time working together, and when we were done shooting movies, someone would inevitably say, "Let's play." And play meant drugs.

I was finally beginning to feel like I had my life together. I was making money. I had my roommates to spend time with. I was going to church and attending affirmations classes during the week when I was in town.

Brenda and Debbie started having problems, and when they fought, they fought. It finally came out that Debbie was sleeping with our landlord's wife. I'd always suspected our landlord, the husband, was gay, and apparently, so was his wife. Brenda and Debbie broke up, which busted up the little family we'd created. We used to go to the Church of Religious Science as a group, but then Brenda didn't want to go in case Debbie was there. Debbie did music for the church, and she didn't want me to bring Brenda when she was performing. *This is church,* I thought, *How can you say someone can't come to church.*

Mikey and I started fighting and his boyfriend, whom he'd met at church, had moved in. We couldn't agree on whether rent should be per person or per bedroom, and I kept eating all their food. Brenda and Debbie called it the cereal wars. When the arguments got ugly, I thought, *This is going to be a mess. I have too much going on. I don't want to deal with this.* I moved into a studio apartment by myself, tipping my balanced life away from friends and family, and into isolation.

Isvara Pranidhana

The Church of Religious Science didn't stick, but I do talk about God a lot in my yoga classes. Sometimes I get e-mails from people saying they can't handle it. Many people have a lot of garbage attached to the concept of God. I don't remember much about Temple. I cut class a lot, and when I was there I was goofing off in the back, often with the chalkboard eraser flying across the room toward my head – I was constantly in trouble. Maybe my disregard for religious studies back then is why I don't suffer at the thought of God the way some people do –

thinking of a Higher Power as damning and condemning, and sending them to hell.

When I was a kid, there was a Lions Club in the town I lived in. Out front they had an enormous statue of a Native American wearing cloaking feathers that came from his head all the way down to his feet. It must have been forty or fifty feet high. I used to think, *Ahh, I bet that's God.* Later, when I found out the bar right next door was a gay bar, I thought, *That's definitely God. He's looking out for us.* When I got clean the first time in the early nineties, someone shared their vision of a Higher Power: Group. Of. Drunks, G.O.D., God. That worked for me for a while.

Now, I don't have an image. For me, God is everything. It's in the people I love and in the people who challenge me, the ones I have thoughts about doing things to other than hugging and loving. You are the image and likeness of God. God is the selfless choices I make. God is the choices I make, and then an hour later think *I can't believe I made that choice. That was selfish, it feels too good; I don't deserve that.* Or, the choices that I know are underhanded or crafty when I do them, and yet act on anyway. God is my good night's sleep, and God is my bad night's sleep. He wakes me up at three in the morning with my bladder that can't hold like it used to.

God is the love I have of my dogs, and the quiet voice urging me, "Can you love all beings like you love your dogs?"

Everything is God. God is LSD, God is mushrooms, God is heroin, God is a junkie with a needle in his arm on sixth and Mission dying tonight on the street. God is everything that's happening with the economy, everything that's happening politically, everything that's happening with people's health, everything that's happening with the environment, whether it's manmade or natural. To me, that is God. All we can do is let it be whatever it is and seek the responsible next right action.

In class, I tell students that if they have any negative connotations with God or any issues around bowing, just make an offering – maybe you call it Krishna, maybe you're comfortable with Christ, or Higher Power, or Universal Spirit, or Divine Spark, or chocolate shakes, or that truth and love in all things. *Isvara Pranidhana* is devotion to the Lord, but anything can be the Lord. Everybody has a Higher Power. Some people just don't know it. Even when I was back out drinking and using, my God – our God – was still there.

When I teach, I devote my students' journey to the Lord. As they go through the *asanas*, poses, I ask them to go emotionally and spiritually to places some of them have never been before. I ask them to do challenging arm balances and to open areas that may be storing trauma. I'm not giving them courage to go there, that's God's work. God is a piece of each of us, that courage and strength is already there. I'm just opening them up to that source and power working in, around, through, and among all of us. It's always there.

Devotion to God is devotion to one another. Devotion means that whatever comes up, we stay connected. If it rains, we take care of each other. When the sun's shining, we take care of each other. When it snows, we take care of each other. If a plane loses the bottoms of its toilets and caca falls on our heads, we're going to take care of each other. Devotion means holding nothing back, no matter how I might look, how I might be perceived, how I might be judged, how I might be denied love. Devotion is saying, "This is me, warts and all."

In recovery, we are encouraged to turn things over to a Higher Power. I don't think I'm any farther away from a drink or a drug than anyone else who's in any recovery program. Just because I went to a meeting this morning, met with my sponsee, talked to my sponsor, and did my prayers or meditation, I still have that switch that can flip. Driving will flip that switch the quickest, especially when someone cuts me off. Much of the maintenance of my spiritual connection is devotion to my Higher Power. If I have the strength to surrender my frustration and road rage, God takes care of it. I love it when people say, "God willing." I always respond, "God is so willing." It's us who aren't always so willing. It's always us.

PART V: AHIMSA

Can you be violent to yourself and non-harming to others without being a hypocrite? Do words and thoughts have the potential to be violent? Is it violence if harm arises from non-action - from refusing or neglecting to act?

Do Re Mi Me Me Me Me...

Before my parents split up, my sister had already found drinking. One night while my parents were out, my sister got trashed and ended up lying on her back at the top of the stairs laughing hysterically. "You know, Mom and Dad are going to be home really soon," I cautioned, "They're going to kick your ass." She started laughing even harder and sputtered, "I don't care." Fascinated by her behavior, I thought to myself, *I want to not care.* That was my first impression of alcohol: an elixir that would allow me to escape the drama, violence, and insanity at home.

For a few years after my parents first split up, my mom insisted that she, my sister, and I go to group therapy sessions together. We'd get so pissed off at each other in those sessions that even though we arrived at the guidance center in one car, when we'd leave, my mom would drive in one direction, my sister would walk in another direction, and I'd walk in yet another. I always went to Burger King to eat. I wanted to block out the experience with a Whopper with cheese (heavy everything), fries, and a chocolate shake. I didn't want to feel anything. As I got older, I discovered there was more than just food and alcohol to numb me out.

* * *

When I found Crystal Meth in LA in 1989, things shifted. Everything started turning toward sex. I would choose to do that over going to the gym, even over working on my tan, so I knew there was a problem. I started partying on a daily basis. In order to fall asleep, I needed to take something like Valium, Halcion, or Flexeril or all of them, and in the morning I'd need a strong coffee to wake me up. If I was in Long Beach, during the day I'd head to the gym, spend some time in the tanning booth, smoke pot or do crystal alone, head to the beach to tan more, and then get ready to go out and party. If I was in LA, I was at the bathhouse or the drug dealer's house. Either way we'd hang out and do drugs. I was always just waiting for my pager to go off. When it did, I often tried to convince my tricks to meet me at the club so I could do my work there, and then continue playing. "I haven't done anything with anyone else yet,"

I would lie. Usually, I had to clean up my act and drive drunk or high to get to their place.

I had my own ads in Frontiers Magazine and the Edge, and I worked through agencies. Ninety-five percent of the calls came from my own ad, and that's the way I liked it since the agency took half of the payment for clients they booked.

There was always a moment of trembling fear before ringing someone's doorbell. If I walked in and saw the money on the counter, that calmed me down. It made it seem like more of a cut-and-dry business transaction. If the money wasn't there, I knew it would get weird at the end. There were some guys who would say afterward, "You definitely just had fun. I shouldn't have to pay you if you had fun." I would reply, "I'm sure you enjoy your job sometimes, too. Just because I have fun doesn't mean you get a hot guy discount. This is just like any other job."

People would hire me for the hour, pay me, we'd do whatever we'd do, and if things went my way I could get out of there in fifteen minutes. I was skilled at that. Once orgasm was achieved, time was up, in my mind. Occasionally people said, "You still have half an hour," and I'd have to stay and cuddle, but that was rare.

I was also good at talking my way through the hour, and making myself sound interesting. Before the client knew it, I'd say, "Okay, hour's up!" When he protested, I would remind him that he hired me for companionship – prostitution is illegal. That was my way of upselling. I knew how to get the most buck for my bang.

Both a chameleon and a master manipulator, I could adapt to fit any situation or adapt any situation to fit me. Some of my tricks would need small talk to relax. I could do that. Many would say, "I've never done this before," and I would assure them, "Don't worry, this is going to be great. I'm a sure thing." Sometimes the door would open and it was on immediately. Although that caught me off guard, I didn't resist it, because the faster it happened, the faster I knew I'd get paid and get out of there.

Some johns I hooked up with were big on doing crystal. Some folks clean compulsively and tinker with projects when they're high on the stuff, but crystal makes many people, myself included, extremely sexual. I could accommodate doing as much blow as my clients offered me. Other guys wanted a romantic evening in front of the fireplace. While one guy was in the shower, I lit candles and moved the flowers in his place around to set a romantic mood. I could do all that stuff no problem, and on short notice. Some guys would call to ask for someone they could dominate, so I'd dress the part and spend the whole drive over getting into character. But when they opened the door, not only would they look nothing like how they'd described themselves, it quickly became clear they wanted to be dominated, not be the dominant one. I was able to identify that and adapt.

Prostituting myself was a different experience from day to day. Some days I'd think, *I'm getting in and out of here*, and I did whatever it took to make that happen. Other days I just wanted to talk, I definitely didn't want to engage in anything else, and I'd stall for the hour. On these days, when people wanted to have relations with me, especially the ones that I didn't really want to spend any time with at all, I would get annoyed. I would treat them terribly, insult them verbally, and that would develop into an abusive sex scene. Those guys always called back for more.

The more I got into meth, the less patient I became about spending time with my johns. And they were the only people in my life at the time. I didn't have friends; I only interacted with people to get money and drugs. I was becoming less and less able to relate to people. Maybe I couldn't consciously relate to my johns because identifying their motivations would have presented me with an all-too-clear reflection of my own state of mind.

Some ridiculously good-looking guys would pay to meet up with me, and I had to ask, "Why do you need to hire someone? What's going on with that?" They didn't really want to hire someone for sex, they just wanted to connect with someone without fear of rejection. Many of them had a social awkwardness that made them uncomfortable being around other people or picking up guys. So to break the ice with someone like me, they would hire me once, develop an intimate connection with me, and then suggest I come back again sometime. For free, they meant. I often crossed that line between business and pleasure. There was always a confused voice in the back of my mind wondering: *Do I want intimacy? Do I want money? Do I want commitment? Do I want independence?* Although I felt the turmoil, I never sat in sober self-study for long enough to recognize how disconnected I was from my *dharma*, my purpose.

I met Kevin at Circus of Books bookstore, "in the back." In reality, it was just a hookup, but at the time I fantasized about turning every hookup into a marriage. Kevin lived in a nice place, and it was clear he had a really nice job. He was super sweet, and super, super cute. He was fun and had a great sense of humor. I moved in with him for about a month. I used to think, *Whatever you want, whenever you want it, I'll do it.* And he was like that toward me too. We had an amazing, magnetic connection. I wanted to love him, and I did love him. But I was so into making money the way I made it that I couldn't commit to him.

He went away on a trip, and while he was gone, I moved out. He could read my intentions so well that while I was packing my belongings, he called from his hotel and said, "You're moving out aren't you."

"Yes," I admitted.

"I can't believe you're doing this when I'm gone." It wasn't that I was trying to hurt him. In truth, I hadn't considered how my different courses of action would affect him. Sneaking out while he was gone was about me and minimizing my own effort, strife, and hardship.

I was great at making up, so when he got back into town, we started dating again. One day, I told him I was going to Washington, DC for a wedding. I was actually going to do a strip job for the weekend. The second night, Saturday night, I got drunk and some guy hired me. He was fat, old, and a smelly smoker. And he wanted to kiss. I kept turning my head to get away from him. I thought, *Is this $500 worth it?* When he left, I lit up a cigarette and started bawling. I called up Kevin, and he asked, "What's the matter?"

"I miss you so much," I sobbed.

"Do you miss me, or do you miss what I represent?"

"Um...?" I wasn't sure how to interpret that.

"What's going on?" he asked.

"I'm not here for a wedding," I confessed. He didn't seem surprised.

"Just come home."

"Okay," I conceded. I was going home the next day anyway.

When I got home, Kevin said, "You have to choose. It's either me and a way of life that's hard for you to figure out. Or you have to do your stripping, and sleeping around, and all this other stuff. You can't have both." And I chose the drugs, and the sex, and the rock and roll. My decision was made partly out of selfishness, but mostly out of fear. If I gave up everything that had become a part of my identity, and then Kevin left me, I would have nothing. I was so scared, and I didn't trust people.

In reality, it was me who couldn't be trusted. I had no basis for trustworthiness. I didn't have any stability, courage, or self-esteem. I had no integrity. My word was no good. I never spent any time thinking, *What do I want to do with my life?* I had no ambition. I just wanted to be high, numbed out. I didn't trust myself. I didn't trust my intuition.

Do you really want to hurt me?

One day, I contacted Bob, and asked if he wanted to have lunch. That was where I was in my life: when I needed someone to talk to, the best choice available was the guy who sent me to jail. He agreed. I went over to his place, and he had this dirtbag of a street kid as a new boyfriend, who was half his age. It was as though I was looking back in time with the clarity of hindsight. I thought, *Oh my God, was I a dirtbag street kid?*

When Bob's boyfriend stepped out to the bathroom, I said unabashedly, "Ugh, I don't want to talk while he's around."

"This is our home that you're in, so get over it," Bob whispered harshly. I was drawn in by his resistance to me.

"I just really miss you. Things just haven't been the same without you. Seeing you again has made me realize that." *Blah, blah, blah,* just like my dad to my mom at my

Bar Mitzvah. But, I finished with a genuine confession, "I think I have a problem with drugs and alcohol." Saying that was humbling and humiliating for me.

"I've seen the work you've been doing," Bob hissed, "How could you do all that? What are you thinking? You're going to kill yourself. You're a mess." He looked over toward the bathroom door, and then leaned in closer to me, "Oh, and you just *want* to have a problem with drugs and alcohol." Before I could respond, the bathroom door opened. I scowled at Bob, and he stared back at me long and hard.

Looking back, all of that was true. How could I do all that? Maybe I did want to have a problem. I knew from attending programs with Bob that there was fellowship and community in recovering from a problem, and I didn't have that. When I went to reach out for help, the one person I had left to talk to was an ex-boyfriend who didn't want anything to do with me or my way of life.

I was lonely, and didn't know how to be around people. I was desperate, but didn't know what to do, I didn't have anyone to talk to. And, I didn't like myself very much. I had moments of reflection when I'd think, *But, I said I wanted all this. Now that I have it, I'm not liking it so much.* There are still things that make me feel like that today. Now, I have the self-control and awareness to sit still and be with that uncomfortable experience. Back then, I didn't know that just sitting with it was an option. I thought I had to do something. I had to act. Or, I had to check out to avoid the discomfort. Drugs and alcohol served that purpose.

Maybe having a drug problem was my way of crying out for a group of people that I could connect with on some level. Maybe prostitution was my way of crying out for a partner I could connect with authentically. Maybe deep down, beneath layers and layers of loneliness, lies, and anger, I was looking for something that would connect me back to myself.

Every now and then, I would actually find that connection. One guy called me to come spank him with a paddle, so I went out to meet him. As I was giving it my best effort, he grabbed the paddle back from me.

"You're not very good at this are you?" he said condescendingly.

"Excuse me?" I was taken aback.

"You suck. I'm paying and you suck at this, and you told me you were good."

"What are you talking about?"

"I'm going to do this to my bed, and however hard you see me hitting, I want you to do it even harder." I winced as he vigorously pummeled his bed. "Do you get what I'm trying to get from you?" I nodded slowly, took the paddle back, and beat the crap out of him.

To paddle him in the way he wanted to be paddled, I had to tap into my deep-seated aggression, anger and self-loathing and channel it with one hundred percent focus into wailing on him. What a release. As I was driving home to Long Beach, a sense of calmness came over my entire spirit. I thought, *Ahh, I'm going to have such a great nap when I get home.*

Just like how an addict in recovery may not have cravings until they pick up a wine glass or a syringe, once I started paddling, I was consumed by it. It took over my mind, body, and soul. In yoga, once the energy switch gets turned on, I can practice for four hours. I sometimes practice vigorously and relentlessly to the point that I collapse into a puddle of sweat for *savasana*, the final resting pose in yoga. It's more than just a physical release, it's an emotional release; something happens to my spirit.

Often amid streaming tears, I am reminded that I get to have teaching and a career because I'm clean and sober. I get to have profound happiness because I have known rage. I get to serve my purpose because I can speak with experience about purposelessness. I get to experience this gratitude because I have been a grandiose, self-entitled motherfucker. Some of the traits I had in my twenties are still inside me, and I need to connect to them in a physical way; in a way I can wring out. I always have my own practice before I teach yoga, because if there's stuck emotions that I haven't worked out during the day, then I would take it out on my students, moving them from pose to pose so quickly that they would scarcely have time to notice what they're feeling. Sometimes you don't know you're paddling until you're paddling. Reining in my aggression so the truth can be unveiled and revealed is part of my ongoing work.

When people make drastic changes in their lives, you hear many of them talk about a burning bush of a spiritual experience. I didn't have that. I didn't get thrown in jail for drunk driving. I didn't black out and run someone over. I didn't have a kid and lose them to the court. It was a series of events that chipped away at me. Every day I sank lower, and became more isolated.

By the early nineties, the drugs were super, crazy out-of-control. The party scene was hard and heavy, and I was using not just daily, but all day, every day. I was even having a hard time showing up for my hustling and porn gigs. If a production company called saying, "Hey, we want to hire you for a scene or two this weekend in Palm Springs," or even if a client called me asking, "Hey, can you be here in an hour?" I would say, "Yes," but I may or may not have actually shown up. I kept getting calls though.

One production company that hired me requested I figure out a way to get flatter abs before the weekend. Back then I was 5'6", weighed about 135 pounds, and had a twenty-seven inch waist, so I was already skinny like no one's business. I went on a four-day speed run, and didn't eat anything until the shoot. Still, all I could do was look in the mirror and think to myself, *Wow, you're really fat.* To numb this sense of inadequacy: more drugs.

From years of using, I'd now learned that getting on a plane wasn't getting away; getting wasted: that was getting away. I wanted to escape my mind and my feelings. All of us look for something to alleviate fear, doubt, and low self-esteem. Drinking and using was that relief for me. There are so many things that people do to deal with these feelings in a responsible way, but I just pushed them away. I'm forty-five, but emotionally I'm in my twenties or thirties because I started cutting off my emotions in my teenage years, stunting my ability to cope with them.

The more I got into drugs, the more I got into the prostitution. The more I got into prostitution, the more I got into drugs. It was a vicious cycle, a downward spiral. I've met people who are recovering from drugs, but continue to prostitute, and I don't understand how they do it. When I was prostituting, I kept thinking I was going to meet someone who'd rescue me from that life. I'd heard about all these guys who had done porn and prostitution, then met a rich guy from Hollywood and settled down with him. Then *Pretty Woman* came out, fueling my fantasies. I thought, "Oh, this is my life story. That's going to be me." Each time that person wasn't the one who was going to rescue me, I had to use drugs that much more heavily. It made me feel awful about myself, having to do something I didn't want to do; something that wasn't of my own choosing; with someone I wouldn't spend time with, someone I wouldn't sleep with, someone I wouldn't even have dinner with. This added to the weight that was dragging me downwards. But I couldn't stop; I didn't know how.

Does That Make Me Crazy? Maybe You're Crazy

My self-esteem issues and discontent were nothing new. I felt that I was in the wrong place, or didn't belong, or needed saving, as far back as I can remember. In February of 1985, after my dad booted me out of his house in Indianapolis and I was back living with my mom in New York, I was hating it. I wasn't enjoying being around my mom or sister, and I didn't have many friends – only the guys I was sleeping with. I never knew how to relate to men unless it was getting in the sack or drinking. While I was still dressed in the Indianapolis fashion of duck shoes, a tie, and two different colored Izods – one with the collar up, one with the collar down – everyone in New York was wearing boots, ratty t-shirts, and jean jackets with Led Zeppelin painted on the back. People often told me I didn't really fit in.

When I started taking Spanish in school, which I was actually interested in, I realized that most of the other students were taking foreign languages only because it was a requirement. None of them could actually speak. From my education in Indianapolis, I could communicate well in Spanish, and the only person I had to talk to was my Spanish teacher. Recognizing that I wasn't happy at this school, she suggested I apply to graduate early using credits from my school in Indianapolis. I was ecstatic to have a ticket out of there. When I told my mom I was going to graduate early and apply for UCLA, she stifled my enthusiasm. She told me I was too young for such a big step, and if I graduated early I would instead attend a local community college until I was eighteen. "My house, my rules," she justified. I felt dejected.

My only solace was a teacher who worked at my school, Mr. Krenner. I don't remember what he taught, but I sure remember what he wore and what he looked like. He was tall with a full head of hair, and he looked wholesome and clean-cut. He was always dressed well and didn't wear a wedding ring, so I was able to create fantastic stories in my mind about him. I imagined that he was exactly the way Joe, my husband now, is and always has been: kind, sweet, and tolerant of someone with uncontainable energy. I was quietly stalking him at the school. I had his schedule memorized so I could walk down certain halls at certain times to make sure I saw him. I even found out his phone number and where he lived. My fantasy was, *He's going to see me. He's going to save me.*

When my mom and sister were out one night and I'd been drinking heavily, I began thinking, *I don't fit in, I'm all alone, I have no friends.* I thought, *My dad kicked me out because I'm gay and my mom hates me because I'm gay. I have no one.* These thoughts began to overwhelm me and took over. I picked up a butcher's knife and sat down at the kitchen table. *Mr. Krenner has never even spoken to me,* I thought, *I have no one. I hate New York, I can't go back to Indianapolis. No one, nowhere, nothing. Nothing to live for.* I sat there gripping the knife tightly, wondering what it would be like to cut into my own skin, to watch the blood gush, to fade in and out of consciousness, to die. *Then would they see me? Then would they care about me?* I sat there staring at the knife. Then my drunken train of thought took a different turn. I staggered over to the phone and dialed Mr. Krenner's number.

"Hello?" he answered.

"This is Les. Les Leventhal," I slurred.

"Who?"

"You don't know who I am?" There was silence on the other end of the line, and my heart sank, "I go to your school."

"Okay," he said hesitantly.

"I'm gay," I came out to him right away, "I've seen you around school, and I think you're cute. I like you. And I just thought – ," I held back tears, "But, you don't even know who I am."

"Listen Les," he said, "I can tell you're going through a tough time, but I'm going to be really honest with you. It would be inappropriate for us to have a relationship in any way. One: your age, two: I'm a teacher, you're a student, so even if you were of age..." He trailed off.

"Oh," I said sadly.

"Where are you?"

"I'm at home."

"What are you doing tonight?"

"I'm home alone." I sighed, "I'm just having a hard time figuring out my life back here in New York. I don't have anyone to talk to. I just can't handle all this any more."

"I know it seems like a lot right now, but things will get better," he comforted me, "Did you just move here? That's always hard."

"It's more than that. There's no reason I should keep going on or bother trying. There's nothing for me. I've been sitting at the kitchen table with this knife..." I admitted.

He continued to talk me down for another half hour. Once I was calmer, he told me he wanted to see me the next day: "Come by tomorrow and introduce yourself," he said, "Let's at least go for a walk and have a talk."

That was all I needed to hear. I brightened up instantly. To me, that may as well have been a marriage proposal. That was how extreme my thinking was: I could go from ending it all to eloping in the blink of an eye. I could hear whatever I wanted to hear. My mind was like Jeckyll and Hyde.

The next day at school, I walked by Mr. Krenner's classroom, but I didn't go in. Half way through my first period, a woman I didn't recognize interrupted the class. "Les Leventhal?" she said, pulling me out of class in the same fashion the administrators would in Juvenile Hall several months later. As we walked down the hall toward the principal's office, she introduced herself in a warm, caring voice as Pauline. I would find out shortly that she was the school counselor. We walked into an office, and sitting inside was the lead psychiatrist for the whole school district. Beside her was Mr. Krenner. And beside him was my mom. *Mmm, I'm in trouble*, I thought. The first thing out of my mouth was, "I didn't do anything wrong."

After we'd all sat down, the district psychiatrist asked me, "How are you feeling?"

"I'm okay," I said, not making eye contact with anyone, "But, I hate being here. I hate this school and I hate New York."

"And how are you feeling about your life?"

"It sucks. I don't like where I live," I reiterated, "I don't like being back here in this school. I don't have any friends."

"And, how are you feeling this morning about suicide?" she segued.

My mom was sobbing by this point. "How could you do this to me?" she managed.

Fuck you, I thought, not even looking at her. *I'm not thinking about you right now. I'm thinking about how I can get away from you.*

They drove my mom and me to the psych ward at a nearby hospital. They walked me around, talking to me in soft, caring tones and asking me questions the whole time.

Finally, I said, "I am not staying here."

"We haven't decided on that either way yet," said the district psychiatrist, "but it won't be voluntary. You're suicidal. We need to hear more from you, and we need to sit down and talk." After spending a good part of the day there, I realized, *If I don't say, 'I do not want to kill myself,' and 'I feel like I have a chance' and 'I can get some help,' I'm going to have to stay in the loony bin.* I figured out what they were wanting to hear and fed it to them.

"We're not going to keep you here," the district psychiatrist finally decided, "but if we suspect one little thing, you're gonna spend thirty days in here with no discussion. Either way, you're going to have to see the counselor at school every day, starting tomorrow." Right in front of me, she said to my mom, "He needs supervision for a couple of days. You need to go home before he gets there and remove everything that's sharp or pointy. Get anything potentially dangerous out of the house." It was humiliating. I thought, *If I want to do it, I'll do it. I'll figure it out. There are tons of places I can go. I can drink a bottle of wine, smash that, and slit my throat if I need to.*

The very next day I started seeing Pauline, the counselor who had retrieved me from my class. She turned out to be a savior for me. The first words out of her mouth were, "Gay, right?"

"Yeah, I think so," I said, not sure what to make of this woman.

"You are or you aren't. Gay? Not gay?"

"Gay," I said with more certainty.

"You've slept with many men, right?"

"Yeah," I confessed.

"Have you ever been with a woman?"

"No."

"Do you want to be with a woman?"

"No."

"You're gay," she said conclusively.

We talked about that for a long time, and then she said, "I want to introduce you to someone."

"Okay," I said hesitantly.

"He can be a friend for you. He's your age, he's out, and he's been out for several years. His family is okay with it. If this is who you're going be, you should have role models in your life. And not people who are in their twenties, thirties, and forties – they can be your mentors – but people who are your age, who you can help you learn how to be who you are now."

"Okay," I said with cautious hope.

My mom didn't know this was going on. The guy Pauline introduced me to came over one day, and when he left my mom said, "What the hell was that?"

"What?" I asked.

"You think you're just going to start dating someone? Having them come over?" The pitch and volume of her voice rose, "And you're going to sleep with someone under my roof? And you're both under age?"

"That's not even what this was about," I snapped.

That did not appease her. She called the school and demanded an explanation. We went back in for a meeting, and Pauline said calmly, "Your son has told us he's gay, and that he likes it, and he's comfortable with it, as best he can be, anyway, with his lack of healthy gay role models. And we want to give him the proper tools and resources to explore his sexuality in a safe way to see if this is how he wants to live his life." My mom crossed her arms and scowled. Pauline continued, "Probably part of his problem has been that he hasn't felt it's okay to explore this." She looked at my mom for a moment, and said, "Are you okay with him being gay?" My mom started crying. She never answered. Which, to me, was an answer.

Ahimsa

In yoga, one of the *yamas* is *ahimsa*, non-violence or non-harming. I've been in too many relationships with physical abuse. Not only with my parents, but also with many of my lovers, there was fighting and punching. Alcohol doesn't make me hit. Drugs don't make me hit. I've been violent my whole life. Whenever "the drugs and alcohol made me do it," the reality was that there were underlying issues so unresolved they had to come out. We are magnets for everything we need in our lives. Of course I was going to meet up with people who were willing to be violent with me.

Physical violence is only one way we harm one another. There are also words and other actions. Throughout my life, many people have reacted to my lifestyle with disgust, disappointment, and aversion, which slowly chipped away at my self-worth. I was harmed and because of that I felt justified passing that harm along to others. I used to say to people, "I've had a shitty day. Good luck." That was my free ticket to take my anger, frustration, or exhaustion out on whomever I was interacting with instead of taking ownership of my mood and actions. That's violence.

It used to be a point of pride that I could deliver backwards, underhanded compliments such that when I walked away people wouldn't know whether I meant "have a nice day" or "f... off." If people questioned me on it, I immediately cleared up the confusion: "In case I wasn't clear, get the fuck out of my life. Your presence is not desired, invited, needed, or wanted. Goodbye." I was skilled at severing ties. That's another form of violence.

Sometimes we trick ourselves into thinking we're being non-violent by being passive-aggressive. This is one of my personal challenges. There are times I realize I said "yes" to you when I should have said, "no," and instead of being direct, I'll act in such a way that you'll get mad at me and you'll leave. You'll be the one to say, "God, you're such a jerk," and make an exit. If you do it, I don't have to feel guilty. Although it's masked by the drama, that's violent, too. Communicating in that way is harmful.

My whole life I've wanted nothing more than to connect with people authentically and to have a community, but my tendencies toward harmfulness, hurtfulness, and aggression actively blocked me from achieving this for much of my life. My violence stemmed from and reinforced my deep-seeded low self-esteem issues. I had no problem putting harmful substances into my body because my internal dialog was so self-critical – someone as worthless as me deserved to be harmed. Using that same rationale I allowed others to harm me – physically, emotionally, sexually – which reinforced my low self-esteem. Taking it one step farther to directly harming myself, contemplating suicide, wasn't much of a stretch.

My tendency for violence persisted into my yoga classes. When I started doing yoga, my practice was aggressive. My teachers helped me develop more grace. Violence has shown up in my yoga teaching, too. I've been the prick who's turned down the music in class, and said, "Okay, we can all hear the phone ringing. If no one wants to get it, I can do us all a favor and chuck it out the window." Now, I realize that people are going to forget about turning off their phones. They've got so many millions of things going on that of course they're going to forget. Phones are going to ring.

Now I can bring things like that up in a more gentle, caring way. When one of the people on a retreat I was teaching kept sneaking off to isolate himself in his room and work on his laptop, instead of getting upset and aggressive, I had a conversation with him, "So, your light was on in your room all night last night. Are you sleeping? Not sleeping? Do you need anything? What's going on?" Rather than dictating what people should do, there's a way to be of service and guide people. In the Yoga Sutras, it says that when a yogi is firmly grounded in non-harming, hostility is abandoned in his presence (2.35). I have seen this happen. When I approach people from a place of love, rather than from a place of aggression, instead of getting defensive, they soften, open up, and are willing to communicate.

Although *ahimsa* is part of my meditation every single day, I don't think I will ever be completely non-harming. Sometimes I don't know how to not harm someone until

I've harmed them. If someone makes me aware that I've hurt them, my intention is to clean it up as quickly as I can. When someone tells me, "I can't believe you said that to me," (sometimes months or years after the offense), instead of getting defensive, feeding more violence into the situation, I try to respond, "I had no idea that was going on. Thank you for telling me so I can respect your boundaries and treat you in more a loving way."

As I've developed a practice of non-violence towards others and gained strength by enforcing non-violence against myself, I've been able to take the practice beyond only non-harming to actually helping people. I'm doing more outreach in the recovery community. I volunteer at a childbirth clinic in Bali. I hold special events in some of my classes that raise money for organizations like Namaste India: Room To Reach and Bumi Sehat in Bali. I never would have imagined I'd be involved in anything like this before my practices of yoga and recovery began to set in and transform me.

PART VI: BRAHMACHARYA

How do you communicate with those you have intimate or sensual relationships with? Do you use sex to connect or to numb out? How would your relationships change if you practiced sex as an act of selflessness and intimacy rather than one of selfishness?

Arabian Nights

One time, one of my agencies set me up with this Sheik from Saudi Arabia who was staying at the Ritz Carlton on Laguna Beach. What a crazy scene. He called back for me night after night. Every evening I'd go down there, and he'd have an elaborate spread of gourmet food, caviar, and champagne. He couldn't bring his pet snakes to America, so he had rubber snakes all over his hotel room to make it feel like home. It was so insane. One night I got down there and the pimp who ran the agency I worked for was there, too. This guy was simply not my type.

"What are you doing here?" I asked, grimacing.

"He wanted to have more than one," he smirked. My skin crawled.

"So, what's going to happen here?"

"He wants us to play with each other."

I was like, "Oh, no. Uh. No. You're not getting a cut of my percentage for this. No. This was not part of the deal." I wouldn't sleep with this guy, even in a blackout but went through with it anyway. That was the job and three bottles of Moet & Chandon helped me through that night. When I couldn't manipulate a situation to fit my will, I manipulated my own thinking to dull the revulsion I felt.

What I know now is that we do not have to prostitute ourselves like this. Whether it's on a street corner, or through an agency. Whether it's sacrificing everything to get a promotion, or bending over backwards to get the prime teaching slot or advertising space at the yoga studio. We prostitute ourselves because we feel we must in order to get by, to be successful, to be happy, to be loved. But prostitution only breeds more prostitution. We don't have to keep doing it. There are other choices we can make, choices that build our self-worth and help us to believe with all of our hearts that we deserve to live with love, to be successful, and to be happy. Yoga is one of these things for me.

* * *

The damage that prostitution had done to my self-esteem became apparent down the road, during my very first sober sexual experience. It was with a guy I actually wanted to be with. We had an amazing long, full day up in Bolinas, just North of the Golden Gate Bridge. We drove out of the fog in San Francisco to a warm sunlit beach. We shared some savory and sweet treats from the Bolinas Bakery and talked about our lives, recovery, slips from recovery, and desires for our futures. Jason was both cute and a good communicator, a winning combination that I had not had in my life for quite some time. After that carefree day, we went back to his place in San Francisco and crawled into bed. I thought, *This is going to be great.* He looked me in the eyes and asked, "What do you want to do?" No one had ever asked me that in my entire life. That choice was never afforded me nor offered to me. It was never my choice. Ever. In that moment, I realized that all the craziness of the drinking and the drugging stemmed from me never actually wanting to sell myself in the first place. I was really trying to find that intimacy. And the more I kept trying to find it, the more people I went through. The more I kept doing that business, the more I had to drink and use to drown out those experiences and feelings.

* * *

When I lived in Long Beach, I met a guy named Charles at the gym. After we'd run into each other a couple times, I ventured, "We should really get together. Have dinner, play, whatever. We should hang out."

"I can't," he replied, "I know who you are, and I don't... I can't... I don't interact with people like you." That cut deep. I felt rejected, thinking, *I'm not different.* My addictive *I don't do 'no'* habit kicked in – I found out where he worked so I could "run into" him there and convince him that we should go out. Just for one night. Just for dinner. After several attempts on my part, he finally conceded.

Before we went out for dinner, I spent a night writing a Harlequin romance-style poem for Charles. If I thought a relationship was on the brink and that I wasn't going to get what I wanted, I could write amazing get-in-touch-with-my-heart-and-feelings letters to suck people in. At dinner I was on my best behavior. My intention was, *I really want to sleep with this guy.* It had nothing to do with genuinely wanting to connect with him or to be intimate with him. I wanted to break his morals and ethics. When he told me he couldn't be with me, I needed to make sure that it happened. *I'll show you,* I thought. *You're going to realize you're missing out on a whole lot of fun in your life because you have these stupid rules about who you are and who you can be with.*

After dinner Charles and I started walking toward his apartment.

"So, we're walking back to your place," I said.

"Yeah, we are," he said without looking at me.

"I think that's great."

"Yeah..." he said hesitantly.

When we got to his place we sat on his bed and talked. I thought, *We're in his bed, and we're just sitting here. I need to pull out the ace up my sleeve.* "I want to read something to you," I said softly. I read him the sloppy, slushy, gooey poem I wrote for him. And then we slept together.

I had to set an alarm for five in the morning to make it to work on time the next day. In the morning, as I reached to turn off the alarm in the dim light, I knocked a glass off the bedside table and it shattered everywhere. When I said goodbye to Charles, he said, "Thank you for letting me have this one experience with you..." in a voice about as broken as the glass I'd smashed, and continued, "But this is it. We can't do this again." Of course, I tried to regain control of the situation and convince him otherwise, but this time he stood firm.

Brahmacharya

One of the *yamas* is *brahmacharya*, which refers to the ideal of celibacy or the practice of responsibility in intimate relationships. It goes without saying that I have some life-long work and healing to do in this department. It seems as if every yoga teacher has a different interpretation of what the practice of *brahmacharya* looks like in this day and age. I've heard people say that sex should only be used for procreating. Obviously I'm not practicing that – if I were, I'd have a wife and kids – but I do today believe in moderation.

A baseline-level practice of *brahmacharya* is to avoid taking someone's boundaries, ethics and morals, crumpling them up like a piece of trash, and jumping up and down on them, saying, "That wasn't what you wanted? Not my problem. Maybe next time you'll pay better attention. It's nice that you have standards, but they've got nothing to do with what I want or need." That was what I did to Charles when I took his "no" as a cue to put even more dedicated effort into seducing him.

Sex can be another one of my addictions: when I first got clean and sober in the early nineties, my sexual addiction was raging. It's how I pushed down and avoided the overwhelming emotions and spinning thoughts that came up when I attended meetings. In order to keep sex from being just another drug, for me, there has to be some practice of *tapas:* discipline, austerity.

Brahmacharya is about more than just quantity. It's about responsibility, courtesy, and respect. I'm a gay boy who's been in relationships, out of relationships, I've played in all sorts of sex clubs, and prostituted myself. In my experience, in all of these situations except prostitution for me, it's possible to practice sexual responsibility. At a sex club, everyone is there for one reason, but people can still hold one another with mutual respect and understanding so it can be fun, stimulating, exciting, joyful, and non-harming. Everyone has a path filled with questions about what is appropriate for themselves, and it is vital that we communicate to understand others' processes and to respect their boundaries.

Sex has some obvious consequences that we all know about, but sometimes we don't consider them truthfully, with *satya.* Sex feels so good that people don't think about the reality of having a baby, raising a child, coping with a teenager, and forever being in the role of parent (whether they remain in the child's life or not). With the advent of wonderful, amazing HIV/AIDS medications, this sexually transmitted virus doesn't seem as scary, and not using condoms has become more prevalent again. But this nonchalant attitude ignores the constant roller coaster of adding, subtracting, multiplying, and dividing several drugs to manage side effects and resistances, which I witness so many people juggle with love and care.

There are more subtle, but sometimes more harmful, waves that sex can create. *Brahmacharya* is a commitment to being aware of the intentions behind my choices. I've told people, sexual or otherwise, "Yes, this is okay," when it wasn't. I've also said, "No this isn't okay," when it was everything I wanted, but I was playing games. *Satya, aparigraha* and *asteya* are missing there: I was lying, unwilling to let go of my power and mistrust, and stealing from someone the opportunity to connect authentically. *Brahmacharya* is about knowing the difference between sex and intimacy, and knowing when I'm playing with one, dancing between the two, confusing them, or pretending to confuse them. It's about connecting on a level that is meaningful and loving. And meaningful and loving can be saying to my partner, "I had a hard day and I would love to relieve some stress. Do you want to come to bed with me?" There's awareness and communication of intention there.

Sexual responsibility is about honoring my partner's willingness and availability, without getting passive aggressive, manipulative, or overstepping boundaries when the answer is "no." I'm skilled at getting what I want when I want it: I know how to sugarcoat things, decorate them, disguise them, and push for them. I'm good at turning "no" into "yes." In many cases there were good reasons for someone to say no, so my manipulation was twice as harming.

This applies in committed relationships, too. Just because Joe and I have been together for fifteen years doesn't mean I get to thrust my desires beyond his availability to connect on that level. If Joe gets home from a stressful day and says he just wants to go to sleep, I have to be mindful and respectful of that, even if I've already picked up the dog poop from the back yard, done the dishes, bought flowers and lit candles. Allowing addictive behaviors like lying, cheating, stealing, and manipulating to take over my sex life would be disrespecting myself and my husband.

Brahmacharya also means respecting the changing shape and form of sexuality as our relationship matures. We've been together for a long time – it's not always an elaborate experience with candlelight, background music, waterfalls, and rose petals like when we first met, everyday. Some days it's as simple as, "Hey, is your animal awake? My animal's awake. What time are you going to be home?" That I can now communicate with someone on that level and have fun with it is amazing. The trust that arises from connecting authentically is the reward for going to the scary, vulnerable place of being open and honest. When I shared my thoughts, feelings, and desires with Joe, I often thought I was just emptying my mind to lift some weight from my shoulders. I didn't realize that was strengthening the bond between us.

PART VII: SANTOSHA

What joys and pleasures do you fight to keep in your life?
Could you be content if you lost them? What discomforts do
you fight to keep at bay? Could you be content if they became a
part of your life?

Vroom Vroom...

Different things started happening in my life that
chipped away at the preconception that I was
untouchable. Once, after spending several days in LA, I
drove back home to Long Beach to restock on drugs.
Living in a tiny apartment at the time, I didn't have much
stuff, but I did have a ton of drugs. It's so funny to look
back. Everybody in recovery says, "Wow, back when we
were using we had tons of money for tons of drugs and
tons of alcohol. And then we get sober and we can barely
figure out how to afford a transit pass to get around
town. How did that happen?"

I didn't live in the best neighborhood in Long Beach,
and by the time I got back out to my blue Hyundai there
was someone sitting inside robbing it. *Oh no you don't!* I
had been mugged once before when I lived with Bob

above the dirty bookstore, and as I marched toward my car, this event replayed in my mind, fueling my anger.

When I'd been mugged the first time, I had been on Santa Monica Boulevard in an area known for rampant prostitution. I got into a car with a cute guy, and he grinned, "You want to play with me, don't you."

"Oh, yeah," I flirted.

"Okay, I'm just going to stop off at my buddy's and pick up a little pot. That will be fun for us."

"Sure," I said. I never understood having sex on pot – my drug of choice was speed – but what the john wanted, the john got.

We pulled up in front of his friend's house, and two guys jumped out from somewhere, got in the back of the car, and pressed a knife to the back of my neck. "Don't move," one of them threatened. As we drove off my heart pounded in my ears. *What am I going to do, what am I going to do?* We stopped at a red light. I glanced over at the driver's side window. It was open all the way. I looked over my shoulder to see how big the knife was. The guy holding the knife growled, "Do not move." I thought to myself, *I have one shot. There's no way they're expecting me to do anything. I have just one shot.* So with every bit of strength, power, and blind courage I had – augmented by a huge adrenaline rush – I flew out the driver's side window and tumbled into the street.

I was shirtless, wearing nothing but my red hot Levis and cowboy boots. One couple leaned out their window and asked hesitantly if I was okay. The muggers had taken all my money. I called the cops, and they were unsympathetic, "What are we going to do for you?" the officer asked rhetorically, "We're going to take you home. That's it." He looked at me sadly and continued, "Stop doing what you're doing. You're a young kid, you don't need to be doing this." I went back home, took a shower, put on a shirt, and was back out on the street an hour later. I had to make up all that money.

I was not about to let the guy sitting in my car in Long Beach set me back like that again. Quiet rage boiling inside of me, I opened the back door of my car, snatched up my club lock, jumped on the roof like Superman, and bellowed, "Get outta my car!" The enormous man stepped out of my car, and evaluated my five foot, six inch frame. He flashed the blade of a knife, and said matter-of-factly, "I win." In an instant, I went from *I'm the man* to *I'm gonna let you keep robbing my car*. I ran back to my house and waited fifteen or twenty minutes. I didn't bother calling the police this time. By the time I got back to my car he'd taken everything. True

Les Leventhal

to my way of doing things at the time, I did some of my drugs, drove back to LA, continued partying.

I had some scary incidents with my johns too. One night I drove all the way to Riverside from Long Beach, which is a good hour's drive, to meet a guy on a secluded ranch. Driving along the broken road, the illumination of my headlights was the only sign of life for miles around. At the ranch gate, I turned off my engine to be met with disconcerting silence. What had I gotten myself into? A young guy came to meet me in his truck. He drawled, "Just leave your car here, and we'll take my truck back to where I'm staying." I remember thinking, *This is friggin' weird.* The drive was probably short, but it felt like forever. The truck slowed, and its headlights illuminated a trailer that looked like it hadn't been moved in years. *Oh my God, this guy lives in a trailer in the middle of nowhere.*

The truck came to a halt. There was a pause. All of a sudden, a masked demon leapt into the headlights, its teeth glowing and its eyes hollow. I yelped and threw my hands up in front of my face, lurching my body back against the seat in a futile effort to escape. It ended up being his dog. The guy consoled me, "It's okay, it's okay. It gets dark out here, and it's probably more quiet than what you're used to. Some people get scared, but it's actually quite nice and peaceful." I tried to get into that. Nice. Peaceful. But then when we got out of the truck, he pulled out a rifle and brought it into the trailer with us. *Oh God God God,* I thought, *This is going to get even weirder.*

It turned out he was one of those people who wanted to talk, talk, talk, talk, talk. And I didn't. I was on edge. I wanted to get it done. I didn't care how we were going to get there, I just wanted out of that place.

Then when the hour was up and we'd had sex, he wanted to cuddle, "You're here already, just stay for the night."

"No sorry, I've got other work tonight," I lied.

"You're going to sleep with me and then go out and do other things?" he asked, sounding hurt.

"It's kinda none of your business what I do with my work. You hired me for an hour. If you want me for four hours or the night, you can hire me for that."

He continued to get more confrontational about wanting me to stay, and it pushed my comfort level to the point that I said, "It's definitely time for me to go," and I got up out of bed.

"No, you're going to stay for just ten more minutes," he firmly gripped my arm.

"No," I yanked my arm away from him, "I'm getting dressed right now and leaving."

As I stepped back into my blue jeans I kept my eyes locked on him. I was acutely aware of where the gun was. He made no gesture to get up, so I said "I'm going to walk back to my car," and, more to assure myself than him, "Don't worry, I know the way." Everything about my body was shaking as I stumbled back to my car in the darkness. Much more clearly than ever before, I thought, *Okay, this is getting out of hand.*

Zoom Zoom...

Around this time, there were a couple of mysterious deaths in LA, specifically in the pornography industry. Rumors were circulating about some guy who was found cut up in bags in the dumpster next to a bar known for us prostitutes. I didn't want that to be me.

My one rule was no one comes over to my house. But, one guy had been calling me for months, and I knew he had a partner, so there was no other set-up for him. Finally I said okay. He was another guy who lingered for a long time. I knew something wasn't quite right. After we'd had sex, he said he was going to the kitchen to get some water. I said, "All right." Then he came back and said he was going to go take a shower. "Okay, fine." But my gut was telling me something was going on.

Once he closed the bathroom door, I walked quietly out to the kitchen to get a knife, just in case things got weird. I discovered the biggest, sharpest knife that I had was missing. *Holy shit.* I picked up the next biggest knife and I stuck it in my robe pocket. *I'm in trouble,* I thought. When he got out of the shower, I remained aware of where his hands were at all times. I made some excuse about how he'd have to leave because I was going out to meet some friends, but he took his time getting dressed and getting his things together. As the tension mounted, there was no doubt in my mind that if he'd made one false move, I would have knifed him. Eventually, he left without a stab wound. In a moment of clarity, I realized my life was at a point where I was primed and ready to go to any lengths to protect myself, which was quite bothersome because I had a nagging sense that some of my paranoia was only in my head. Meth will do that to a guy.

I knew something was wrong with my life. I was miserable. I had no friends. I wasn't talking to anyone. What could I talk about? "I'm a hooker, I'm a drug addict, I do porn." There's not much else to say from there. It was unfulfilling craziness. "I kept trying to go back to school, but every time on the first day, I would end up cooped up in the bathhouse twisted out on drugs instead." There aren't many places the conversation can go. If people asked me what I liked to do, the answer was, "Got drugs?"

There was nothing for me on holidays; I was alone. And I remember thinking, *I'm twenty-three years old. I'm gay in LA, which is supposed to be one of the best towns in America to be gay in. And my life still sucks.* I was in California – my whole entire dream come true – and I wanted to die again. I remember that feeling. I didn't have the bravery that I did back when I was sixteen – that bizarre moment with the butcher knife. I didn't have the guts to do something that bold and intentional now. Looking back I understand that drug use was the weak, chicken-shit way of a slower suicide. That's where I was headed.

In the spring of ninety-two, I would go off on three-, four-, five-day speed runs, do a lot of X, and practically live at the bathhouse. I connected with a guy there, and we would hang out together often. Over the span of five days we were going back and forth: his house, the bathhouse, his house, the bathhouse. I can't even tell you what night of the week this was, but I do remember it was around midnight when we got to the bathhouse. He got us a room downstairs so we could do stuff. It was always humid down there; we used to call it the swamp. I was messed up, and according to my drugged-out perception there were maggots crawling out of the walls. And there were people – all of a sudden the ceiling opened up as if there was a trapdoor up there, and there were people with cameras filming us. My eyes darted between the worms wriggling out of the wall and bright lights and the boom mic of the videographers above. I started to feel overwhelmed and woozy. I couldn't bear it any longer. I said, "I don't think I can be here. We have to go." Once upstairs, I got dressed, and sat on the bench to wait for him. I remember the front desk guy saying, "Les, you look like you need some help." I don't remember much else from that night.

I vaguely remember being in his car. I vaguely remember getting back to his house. The next thing I remember is me, in a pair of boxer shorts, running, barefoot, down Santa Monica Boulevard, my arms all scratched up and bleeding. I remember searching frantically for the cops, and once I found them, dragging them back to the guy's place. The cops stopped me at the doorstep, "Uh, before we go upstairs, can you tell us what we're going to find here? What the hell's going on?"

And I said, "The guy has a gun and he's got my parents inside." That's what I was thinking. That's where drugs took me. The guy opened the door and the cops said to him, "You know this guy?"

"Yeah."

"Do you have something to put him to sleep for the next twelve to fourteen hours?"

"Yeah."

"Can you give it to him?"

He agreed. The police left me there, and the guy gave me some downers. I woke up an hour later and told him I was fine and I was leaving. I never spoke to him nor saw him again. To this day I have no idea what I got scratched on. Where did the story about my parents being held at gunpoint come from? Were we messing around with a gun? Maybe that was another one of those moments that could have been the end for me. The last moments of my life could have been spent completely checked-out, numb to reality.

Crash Bang Boom

I knew my life was a complete mess, but I didn't know what I was supposed to do about it. I don't know how this story would have ended if it hadn't been for my friend Tony from San Francisco.

Back in 1989, I had gone up to San Francisco to perform at a couple of strip clubs. While there, I met Tony, who had come to every one of my shows. We weren't each other's type, but he recognized I was looking for a friend, that I was longing for a connection with people. Even though he came to all my shows, he never wanted to sleep with me afterward. We'd just spend time together, eating sushi and drinking lattes. We met up again when I was in San Francisco a year later and decided to go on a trip to Reno together. We had fun, so we went on a few more trips together. One time when we were there I won $6,000 on the slots and then blew all that on a fab trip to London. We became great friends.

He came to visit me in Long Beach in 1992. He didn't usually do a lot of drinking or drugs, but I was a master at peer pressure. I continually convinced myself I didn't have a drinking or drug problem because I shared everything. "Real drug addicts don't share their stuff," I would say, "They tell you they don't have anything and then go do it all on their own."

Tony and I did some ecstasy before getting in the car to head off to a sex club in LA. As we were driving up the 710, the Long Beach Freeway, we passed a huge accident.

He was a nurse and he always carried a pen that could be used to puncture someone's throat if they couldn't breathe. The accident had just happened, and he said, "We have to stop." I glanced over at him, then at the mess in the rear view mirror, and then back at the road ahead. "We're high. We're high and we have a lot of drugs on us. We're not stopping." He tried to convince me to turn around, imploring me to tap into my sense of morality. But I kept driving straight. At that point, I didn't have morals. I had ethics: if it benefited me, then it was ethical. I'd lie, steal, cheat, hurt, and neglect to get what I needed. I had no consideration for other people. Despite Tony's attempt to convince me otherwise, I repeated, "We can't stop. We cannot stop."

They say there's a small percentage of the population who won't ever catch HIV. That's such a dangerous thing for someone like me to hear. In my late teens, especially in West Hollywood, I thought, *Whatever, I'm eighteen years old. How's something like that going to get me?* I was so checked out that I didn't see much press about the disease. I had no education whatsoever.

Tony was a nurse at SF General. It was packed with people who had AIDS. It was the only place taking them in. Tony recognized I was living a high-risk lifestyle, and when I began showing symptoms of cryptococcal meningitis, an infection people with HIV are susceptible to, he insisted I get tested. On one of my trips up to San Francisco, he squeezed me in for some tests. It took weeks for the test results to come in, and in that time, I began living as if I knew I had HIV. I told everyone that I'd been up to San Francisco for these tests, and that I was dying. I told my mom and she was devastated. She began attending support groups for families affected by AIDS. I cried to Kevin, "I'm dying, I'm dying," hoping his pity would get us back together again after I'd ended our relationship, choosing drugs and prostitution over him.

Finally the doctor called me with the test results.

"Everything was negative," she said bluntly.

I paused, "What?"

"You tested negative for HIV. You don't have AIDS," she said.

"But..." I trailed off.

"Get off the drugs," the doctor said.

I gasped, taken aback. *How could you?* I thought.

She continued, "That's why you have all these symptoms. It's from speed and whatever other shit you're doing."

"Thank you for letting me know about my test results," I said curtly, and hung up the phone. I didn't tell some people about the test results for years. I didn't tell my mom until I made amends to her as part of my recovery. I never told Kevin. He died thinking I had AIDS.

The cycle of insanity that I was caught in has killed so many people. There's no reason that I shouldn't have HIV or AIDS. There's no reason I shouldn't already be dead. I used the lambskin condoms that were popular in the eighties with one guy I dated. When it came out that they were terrible, semi-permeable, and stuff got through them all the time, we stopped using condoms altogether. He's dead now, too. I thought, *Oh well, whatever, I've probably got it already with all the things I've been doing.* There were so many times with so many people. Giving and receiving. It's unbelievable that I'm alive and healthy.

San Francisco Blues

Tony could see how out-of-control my life had become. He insisted I come to San Francisco with him to get me out of the environment that was slowly killing me, "Your life is falling apart and it's getting very messy," he said, "No one wants to find you dead." That got through to me. Images of a chopped up prostitute in a dumpster, johns with rifles and knives, and the patients

I'd seen dying of AIDS at SF General flashed through my mind. It had become painfully clear that continuing to live my lifestyle was choosing to die young and painfully. I ran off to Nashville for one final stint of sex, drugs, booze, and money. Then, the day after I got back, I drove up to San Francisco. I swore I would never make that brutal drive again. However, years later, I would drive that same road to get to and from my first yoga teacher training.

Tony's answer to helping me down off daily crystal use was to supply me with Ativan, Halcion, Flexeril, and Valium. I was never a downer kind of guy, but if I mixed alcohol with all that, *Mmm*. I became a downer kind of guy. As if I had a checklist, I started doing all the things I was supposed to do to clean up my life. I got off crystal, got a job, got a boyfriend. I was great at the job I got in the legal department of an aircraft leasing company. Somehow I intuitively knew not to mess it up. But, even though I did all that, many aspects of my life got worse, instead of better. My temper, my dissatisfaction, my low self-esteem, all of these got worse. What I didn't realize at the time was that drug abuse and all that other external stuff are just symptoms of the underlying problems. Although my life looked great on the outside, I hadn't changed anything inside.

When I first moved to the Bay Area, I also applied to be a sheriff for the city and county of San Francisco. It had decent salary and had amazing benefits. Tony said, "You're young. Do this for twenty, thirty, forty years, and look at the retirement you'd have." The first interview was a written test, and they actually called me back for a second interview. But they needed me back on a Tuesday at two in the afternoon. My job at the aircraft leasing company had just gone from temporary to permanent, and I couldn't tell them I needed to leave for a few hours to go get another job. I told the sheriff's office I couldn't make it and let go of that aspiration.

Much later, I found out there was a guy brand new to recovery who saw me in line on the day of testing for the sheriff job. He'd been going through some self esteem issues, thinking, *How can I be here? Who am I to think I deserve a job like this?* He recognized me from my "modeling career," and seeing me in that line shifted his thinking. He recounted his train of thought to me years later: *If you can be here and stand in this line and hold your head up high, I can have the courage to be here, too.* Of course I didn't have my head held high, I was standing there surviving, just like he was.

When he told me that story, I became more aware than ever that no matter what I'm doing, I never know who's watching and receiving hope, help, courage, strength, and support. This was a rare example that someone happened to tell me about. I share this life lesson with my yoga students when they're gripping and straining to stay balanced in a pose like *natarajasana*, dancer's pose: "Some days balance is meant for other people. Practice *aparigraha*, non-greed. Instead of desperately grasping for the pose, can you let yourself fall when it's time to fall? Maybe your falling will be an act of service to someone else in the room who needs permission to fall too."

It wasn't so smart of me to move to San Francisco to get away from my reputation in pornography. Everybody knows. The first Halloween I was there, I was at the Lookout Bar, a popular Castro gay boy bar, with Steve, an aerobics instructor I was dating. He couldn't help but notice the curious glances I was getting from men around the bar. He couldn't handle it. It freaked him out. He used to tell me how disgusting I was and what an awful person I was. He'd continually tell me I'd made bad decisions and that I should be humiliated. And, I was humiliated. I already believed all the stuff he was telling me. I already had all that inside. It didn't help that he was underlining, and **bolding**, and *italicizing* it. The shame was already there, but I didn't know how to do anything about it.

Even then, I thought, *I can't help who I am or where I am.* But, I had no self-esteem. So, I didn't trust that thought, I didn't listen to it. I always had to be around someone in a dating capacity or a sexual capacity to tell me how I felt. I didn't know how I felt. It made it all the more confusing that at the same time as this guy was dating me, sleeping with me, and telling me he loved me, he was trying to change me to fit into the mold of what he thought was presentable. I struggled to process the complex message: *I love you, but I'm trying to change you.*

Steve was a total drunk. We were drunks together. I always surrounded myself with people who looked like me, or were worse. That way it didn't seem like I had such a huge problem. We'd go up to Lake Berryessa every single weekend and get shitfaced. Reverting to my teenage shenanigans, we'd break into people's trailers, steal their pot, and get high. Every other week, Steve and I would break up and then get back together. Then things got messy. He got messy. He had a guy die of a massive heart attack in the high-impact aerobics class he taught. That weekend, we went up to Berryessa like we always did, and after a nice dinner, a few drinks, and two of the Valium he'd been prescribed to help him cope, he passed out. This was no fun, and I was pissed. I thought, *I want one of those Valium, too. I want one!*

I scoured the trailer. *Where the fuck would he hide the bottle?* I thought, *Maybe they're outside. No, there are too many raccoons, or other animals that would get into them. Damn it, where are they?* Just when I thought I had no chance of finding the Valium, I looked up at a little door to a small storage space. I gasped, *Aha, finally! There they are.* I opened the door and grabbed the bottle that Steve had obviously hidden. I wrenched off the cap, and pills scattered everywhere. That was my biggest moment of clarity. With scattered Valium around my feet, I thought, *Just look at how desperate I am.*

Steve and I got in a huge fight on the drive home and broke up again. That didn't last long. The following weekend he called me up and slurred, "I'm on my way home. I need to stop by."

"You're drunk," I stated, "Are you driving?"

"Yeah."

"Don't drive." I said firmly.

He hung up the phone and showed up at my house about an hour and a half later in a complete blackout. He was so wasted he couldn't even complete sentences. He had no idea what we were talking about. He didn't even know where he was or what he was doing. I knew he wouldn't remember anything I said, "Well, I guess I have to let you stay here now. I don't know what to do with you."

The weekend after that, he was up at Berryessa by himself. He supposedly slipped and fell into the fire and burnt the whole left side of his body. *Oh my God*, I thought. *He was drunk and fell into the fire. That could just as easily have been me.*

I've had my fair share of stuff. I've been in jail. I've had some close calls. I've driven drunk. I've driven high. It got even worse during my three-year relapse. But the universe has always provided more severe signs with other people to wake me up: *This could be you. This is what's out there waiting for you.*

I was the common denominator of all these different events crashing down around me. And I was so unhappy. I'd run away from so many places, so many people, and so many things that there was no one around to be angry at. Even though I was so angry, I was so alone. Maybe it wasn't the people I'd run away from who had been the problem. Maybe there was no place I could run away to that would be the solution. I was the problem.

When I was drinking and using nonstop, I couldn't have any emotion. But there would be these moments in which I'd wake up. I knew the jig was up when I was watching General Hospital, and Robert Scorpio's boat blew up, and he died for the seventh time. I cried. I thought, *Why am I crying? When was the last time I cried?* Then I realized, *Something's not right. My life's a mess.* I didn't want to be alone any more. I thought, *Some people have boyfriends, some have girlfriends, some people are getting married. How come I can't find anybody?*

I already knew the answer. I'd run away enough times to realize that changing locations would not change my long-standing problems. I had to do something about me. About my lifestyle. My other option was to continue drinking and using until I died.

Santosha

I've had a gifted life. I got to have so much life in forty-five years. Some people live until eighty and won't have as much life as I had up until I was twenty. I'm grateful I got to have a life at all. More than once, I've been to the dark place of thinking, *What's the point?* And, I've been afforded a second chance. Many people are not so lucky.

There was a guy I dated when I got into the program in the nineties, and when we both relapsed we hooked up again. He never made it back into recovery. His heart gave out when he was thirty-four years old. On the same day, another guy I knew blew his brains out. And then the next week another guy in his early thirties overdosed. Then a week after that, another kid who'd been in and out of recovery killed himself too.

These stories are heart-breaking, and they're sobering reminders that just because I have spent time in recovery, doesn't mean that can't happen to me. I know where the disease can take me. I'm not immune. Sometimes when I think back to my lifestyle in LA, I have the peculiar mental twist that makes me wonder, *What would have happened if I'd stayed? Should I go back?* This is why I go to recovery groups: other people's experiences remind me that those first few months in LA were a scramble. I was in survival mode, scratching and clawing to get by. Now that I'm in recovery I know I never have to go back to that way of living. No matter what happens in my life, my worst day sober is still better than when I was back there running around like a maniac.

Going to meetings also reminds me of how grateful people are when they find recovery. It's easy to forget how grateful I was when I first came in. One of the *niyamas* is *santosha*, contentment, and for me, contentment is rooted in seeking gratitude.

I'm grateful that I get to experience the *asana* limb of yoga, the poses, even if it's sometimes through watching others do things I can't. I'm grateful I have a yoga mat; I'm grateful that if you need a yoga mat, I have an extra one you can use. I'm grateful that I have a studio to teach at, and that other studios around the world want me to come teach. I'm grateful that not only do I have a partner, I've had the same one for fifteen years. At one time, I was content just to have someone for the hour and make a few hundred bucks.

However, contentment and gratitude don't come naturally to me. I have a bizarre mental tic that makes me believe that all I have isn't enough. *Santosha* is a daily practice of reshaping thoughts: *Thank you that my lower back has been bothering me for a month. Thank you for letting me know I have a lower back; some people have fused vertebrae and can't bend at all. Thank you for my tight hamstrings; some people don't have legs.* When I faced challenges in my life, I used to look at myself as the victim and think, *I can't believe this is happening to me.* Now when I look at my life, I can't believe more things haven't happened to me. What I feel is beyond contentment, it's gratitude.

I'm so grateful and excited that I'm turning forty-six. I think, *Wow, I lived until forty-six.* I remember feeling like it would be okay if I died. I was sixteen when I thought, *I'm done. Here's the knife. Let's go.* That could have been it, I would have missed out on all I've experienced since. There's thirty extra years. Every breath now is a bonus, not without challenges some days, but still, it's a gift.

Many people worry that as they age no one will pay attention to them, they'll be all alone. We live in a culture focused on youth and all the things we can do to maintain that. The message is, *There's always something to improve about your body. Always.* That was accentuated in the pornography industry. The thought is, when you're young, cute, and you have the body, people will want to be with you. But, as I've gotten older, I have found out intimacy is about so much more than physical appearance. Some people don't find that out. Some people die too soon. Some people kill themselves.

Sometimes yoga is presented as a cure-all that will keep you looking and moving like a twenty-year-old until you're sixty or seventy. We seem to think that if we can maintain the appearance of youth on the outside, it can get crammed in to the inside. Or, we think that if we can do challenging poses, it will "yogafy" our mind and spirit. That's not how it works. Just as drug and alcohol abuse are just symptoms of inner turmoil, a beautiful *asana* practice is a projection of our interior landscape, not the other way around.

At a workshop I taught, a student got into *Dwi Pada Viparita Dandasana*, quite an advanced backbend, for the first time. They immediately asked, "What do I do now? What do I do next?" I said, "Just breathe. *Santosha*, contentment. Maybe you're just meant to be here. Just breathe and just be." It was such a reflection of how discontented we can be with the present moment. We see something we want, then, when God gives it to us, we look for something else, usually more. Go ahead and enjoy your gift as it's presented.

One of my biggest challenges when it comes to contentment and gratitude is my relationship *to* money, *with* money, *for* money, and *without* money. That relationship is a huge force in other people's lives and in my own. I lived in a time when the economy was booming and a sales career was successful. *We're going to be millionaires*, I thought as I made investments for Joe and myself, planning to sell them at the peak of the boom. I thought, *Then, we'll be happy*. When the stock market crashed, I became obsessed with how we were going to recover our losses so that we could still be millionaires. It took a lot of yoga, but now I am content that we have what we have. I recognize now that I have abundance in my life. I'm no longer making, re-making, and making-over charts of how much money I have now and how much I will I need to make to retire at fifty-five, sixty-five, sixty-nine, seventy, seventy-three, seventy-five... In my mind, I am retired now. I just happen to teach yoga in my retirement.

As a yogi, it's important for me to not chase my first yoga experience. Some of the layers of specialness and sacredness that used to surround yoga have melted away for me but new layers have been revealed. Part of my practice of meditation is to learn to be okay with that. I did my first yoga teacher training with Ana Forrest in 2005, and I'll never again go through that exact same preconception-shattering, life-changing journey. It's important for me not to go into my continuing education courses trying to recapture that experience. If I did, I'd miss out on this stage of the journey.

A studio that I taught at wasn't always happy that I travel so much, that I'm not pulling the big numbers in classes that I used to, and I imagined they wanted me to go back to being the ruthless salesperson I used to be. I can't help but think, *Wait. The yoga's working. I can't go back now, I want to see what happens next.* We can choose to stay stuck in familiar patterns of destructive behavior, or we must learn to find contentment in riding the waves of change. Sometimes it can be easier to stay stuck in a decorated rut than walk through the fear-inducing door of change, but on the other side of that door there is unimaginable opportunity.

Les Leventhal

PART VIII: SAUCA

Do you acknowledge your unfiltered, raw thoughts even if they aren't pretty? Is your self-expression clear or inhibited? What are people around you missing out on because of what you're holding back?

So Young So Sober – Sort Of

It was February of ninety-three when I stepped into my first recovery program meeting *for me*. There was no one telling me I should go, there was no one saying, "You know, you might want to check this out." I was going for me. I picked a meeting in the Castro district of San Francisco because I knew it would be mostly guys, and because it had a break, I knew I could bail if I needed to. I took a Valium before I drove over. I lived in Hayes Valley, which is only a five-minute drive from the Castro, but I left an hour early. When I got there, the door wasn't open yet, but there was a guy standing outside. I leaned against the wall of the building and crossed my arms.

"How long have you been clean and sober?" he asked conversationally.

"Huh?" I was taken aback by the forwardness of the question.

"When was the last time you had a drink?"

"Four days ago," I said matter-of-factually.

"What about drugs?"

"What kind?" I hesitated.

He tilted his head down and looked up at me through bushy eyebrows as if to purposely add dramatic effect, "Anything."

"Well, I took a Valium to get here so I could be kind of calm and relaxed. I'm nervous."

"So, you're not clean."

You asshole, I thought. I went into the meeting feeling resentful right off the bat, and when the break hit, I was outta there. It was too much community and support all at once. People wanted to get close and were interested and caring. But when I got home, it dawned on me, *Isn't that what I want, even though I don't know how to connect in that way?*

I went back about a week later. Then again. Then some more. It was scary at first and it was hard because I didn't know what I was doing there, and even though I'd been around recovery programs before in LA, I didn't know how this was going to turn out. Was I going to have to stop forever, or could I learn to, as I always used to say, "I can learn to drink like normal guys" and "Use socially." Just a little social heroin, a little social crack.

I started meeting people in the program and hanging out with them a bit. They always say, "Don't date the newcomer." We have so much going on, and to be objectified sexually is the last thing we need, especially since I had healing work to do around sex and sexuality. But when I met Tom, there was something about the way he held me, made me naively believe, *It's going to be okay.* Tom was in his late twenties or early thirties, tall and handsome with a lush head of hair, just like Kevin's. One of the things that made him irresistible to me was the way we connected when kissing. He would pull back from a crazy, passionate kiss, gaze into my eyes, and say, "Oh. My. God." It made my body, mind, and spirit electrify and explode to have someone respond to me like that. Today, I often experience this same feeling on my yoga mat. I am able to channel the love that comes about in my own practice into offering students the possibility of dancing and playing at their physical, emotional, and spiritual edges on their mats when I teach. If I'm having this experience, I know others can, too.

On my sixty-day sobriety anniversary I was supposed to go to a meeting to get a chip. But I didn't go. In fact, I planned not to go. I planned to relapse. I bought two bottles of white wine, put them in my refrigerator, then, drove to Japantown and sake'd myself into a frenzy. I don't know how I drove home and didn't wreck the car. The bottles of wine from my fridge were empty the next morning, so I must have finished them both. I vaguely remember Tom coming over and putting a trash basket next to me, and I clearly remember puking into it.

The next morning my phone rang. It was my mother.

"What do you want?" I moaned.

"I hope you're feeling a great big hangover. I'm your wake-up call. Get to work, asshole."

I had called my mother in a blackout the night before. *Oh my God.*

I went to Tom's house that night, and he said, "You know we can't do this any more." My heart sank. I knew he was right. I had broken my commitment to recovery and expected Tom to come take care of me, putting his own recovery process at risk. Still, it was one of the saddest moments in my life. In that moment, all of that desire for someone to fix me, to rescue me, to take care of me was gone. I knew I had to take ownership of my problems. I was the only one who could save me.

172

Tom sent me to a friend, Lon. I went to his house and sat silently on his couch. Eventually he said, "Let's talk about it."

"I don't know what to say," I sighed, "I don't know what happened. I'm just so, so, so hungover and sick right now." Eventually, I revealed how I'd consciously chosen to relapse.

Lon introduced me to a guy affiliated with an outpatient recovery program called Eighteenth Street Services, which unfortunately no longer exists. I did that three or four times a week for the next six months. There were group and individual sessions. The hardest part of the program was the group social we were supposed to plan. We couldn't figure it out. Our counselor tried to help us along, suggesting we do something for just half an hour after our group session one night. "Just nine fifteen until nine forty-five," he offered. We stared at him blankly. "From nine fifteen to nine thirty?" he coaxed. Finally one of the guys suggested going to the Glass Coffin, which is everyone's nickname for a bar that's all windows and used to be full of super old men. I don't even remember what its real name is. We got there and stood around uncomfortably, "This is the most fucked up thing," I grumbled to a guy I knew, "We're all in recovery and we're at a bar." I ordered a coffee, and it came in a brandy snifter. I rolled my eyes, "I can't drink this," I told the bartender haughtily, "I have stemware issues." I gave up on the group social and left.

It was an edgy time. I didn't know from day to day if I was going to stay clean. I was getting up in the morning, walking my black lab – Honey – who I'd adopted from the SPCA, going to the gym, going to work, and going to a meeting at lunch time. At nights I had either group or individual counseling. Those sessions were always over in time to get to a meeting as well. I was going to two, sometimes three, meetings a day. Definitely three on weekends. At the end of the day, I'd crawl into bed, and Honey was just there to love me. She was a great teacher. I've never cried so hard as the day Honey passed in 2000. My tattoos are all about my dogs and family, a tribute to love and community.

The good thing and the hard thing is that getting into recovery doesn't change anything overnight. Even today, there are things that make me think, *Oh wow, I still have work to do.* But thank God I still have work to do. For one, I get bored if there's nothing to do. But more importantly, I've noticed that the things I haven't worked for are no longer in my life. I took them for granted and lost them. If I've had to put effort and persistence into something, I value it, and it's more likely to remain in my life, like my crazy, deep love for Joe.

When I encounter people who have been abused, my hope is that they are going places, seeing people, and doing the work to come around. Not everyone wants to do the work, but I am so grateful for the work I have done and continue to do. It reminds me that I care about other people, not just myself. I moved from humiliation to humility. What a gift. You can call that yoga, you can call that recovery, but knowing where I came from, I call that a miracle.

When my group graduated from the Eighteenth Street Services program, we had to talk about how we were going to fill our free time. We each had a goal and a vision of action that we had committed to accomplish. By that time, after a few months of sobriety, I'd realized what a butthead I'd been to my family. I wanted to make them happy. My goal was to go back to school: to get my GED, and start going to college. So I did that. One of the first classes I took was Human Sexuality. I thought I'd pass it with flying colors with my experience, but it was one of the hardest classes I've ever taken as the content was nothing what I thought it would be.

I went through a period that they call a Pink Cloud. It's a period of positivity when all the work we do in recovery begins to pay off. I got on a Pink Cloud, and I didn't get off it for a long time. The danger of a Pink Cloud is that when we start to see benefits, we're less motivated to keep doing what it took to get them in the first place. I flitted and floated around and stopped doing the work. My life got good on the outside, but just as my parents presented their marriage in a way that looked good to people outside our immediate family, my accomplishments masked the self-esteem issues that were still eating away at me.

When people say, "I have a drinking problem, I have a drug problem. I'll quit and my life's going to get really good," I say, "No, drinking and using are just some of the symptoms. You were drinking and using for a reason. What was going on? What's underneath all of that?" For some people it's years and years of issues that are not going to unwind in a single yoga teacher training or even a solid year of yoga practice. It could take the rest of a lifetime. I'm thirteen years clean and sober (this time around), and there are still things I'm just discovering.

When I went back to school, I was still working at the aircraft leasing company. I was there for a few years, which was the most stability I had in my entire life. I was doing some homework there one day, and a woman I worked with asked me, "What are you doing?"

"Astronomy," I said.

"Oh," she said, "How's it going for you?"

"It's fun, but the teacher is super hard."

"Are you going to be an astronaut?" she asked.

"No."

"Are you going to be a teacher?"

"No"

"Well, what do you want to do?"

"I don't know," I admitted.

"You should go into business management school. You could get into sales and stuff and work at a company like this," she suggested.

"I can't do that," I protested, "I don't have the time or the money."

"Here's the deal," she said, "I know you're in recovery. I'm in recovery too. I'm a single mom, I have three kids, I work full time, and I go to school at nights. So what's your excuse?"

Who is this woman? I thought, *Get her out of my life.* I didn't like someone calling me out on my excuses, but she was right and I knew it.

I ended up going to night school at the University of Phoenix. I did a super accelerated business program, in which there was a new class every six to eight weeks. We had group presentations, individual presentations, and tests every week. You'd finish one class on a Monday night with a final exam. At the end of that class we'd get our books and a list of homework due for our next class, which started the following Monday. We hadn't even met our next teacher, so if we had questions, we usually had to ask them after we turned in our assignments. It was great training for lots of things. In some ways it was completely nuts, but it provided structure for me, and I needed structure in my life. Free time was dangerous.

As I progressed through school, I transitioned from secretaryship to contracts to sales. Because I was doing a business program, I talked to the companies I got jobs at into paying for parts of my education. I was a natural salesman. When one company made me an offer, I negotiated that if they increased my salary and put me on the fast track to move into sales then it would cover my education. They bought that.

Even my relationship with my family was improving. My mom and I talked on the phone regularly, although I don't think we'd have much to say if we weren't gossiping about other family members. She was proud of me for going to school. As I madly worked all night to finish essays and sweated through final exams, I thought, *I'm finally making everyone happy.*

By the time I graduated in the spring of 1997, I was working as a salesperson at the aircraft engine leasing company. I was already traveling a bit, but not too much. My graduation was a huge deal. I even took myself on a whirlwind tour of Spain as a graduation present. My mom and sister came out to California to show their support, and the whole recovery community came out for a party I had. I fit 125 people into my tiny railroad apartment in Hayes Valley. The recovery community is amazing in that way. If you need support with something because it's a terrible experience, they're there. If you're celebrating something, they're there.

My cousin had a brunch after the actual graduation in San Jose, and I was so tired that I snuck into one of the bedrooms, and took a nap. Drifting off to sleep, I thought, *Now, finally, everyone should be happy.*

I'm So Smart I Can Balance The Unbalanceable

When I graduated school, my sales career immediately sprang to a new level. I started traveling constantly for work. I was putting money in the bank like no one's business, and that felt amazing. It wasn't only the money that was motivating me, it was chasing the deal. I was driven to pursue, schmooze, negotiate, and conquer.

Back when I lived with my dad in Indianapolis I used to go out to Holiday Park, where men would go to have sex. One night when I was there, I ran into the father of one of the boys I coached swimming to. *This is hot*, I thought, *I definitely want to do this.* He was visibly uncomfortable with the inappropriateness of our encounter given my role in his son's life, the age difference, the lack of anonymity. I, on the other hand, was thinking, *This is right up my everything-is-wrong-about-it alley. We have to do this.* It took all my charm to convince him to play, but eventually he caved. It was amazing. It didn't matter if the sex was good or not, it was all about the chase. It was the same way when I was a salesman. Their signature was my orgasm. Once I actually got it, I lost interest.

I knew how to get things started. On a business trip I'd make a phone call: "Hey, I'm down in Argentina, I heard you guys were thinking of doing something with your engines in Chile. I'm coming over, and I'm going to spend an extra week. Let's just talk and have lunch. We'll brainstorm ideas and see what we can come up with." I was great at doing presentations. I had engines and I knew how to convince people they needed them, even if they didn't even own any airplanes yet.

Just like when I worked as a prostitute, I was still a chameleon. If you represented the airline, I knew how to talk to you like an airline employee; on the phone with the bank, I knew how to fit in there too. Once I'd worked out a creative deal with a client, I'd call up the bank: the technical team, the attorney, the finance guy. Usually it would work out, but sometimes my boss would call me back and veto my proposed deal. Working my salesman techniques on my own company, I'd say, "It's ten frickin' engines. Ten engines. Do you want this to go to the competition or not? Just say yes or no. If you want this to go to the competition, I'll get on the plane and come home right away. I'm missing home. If not, I'll stay down here. What do you want to do? How are our numbers for the quarter and year?"

Behind my veil of confidence, I felt like a phony. Whenever I showed the clients a model or a graph, I'd worry they'd ask me a question I didn't know the answer to. When I called up the bank to get approval for a deal, I dreaded the day they'd fire me for making a ridiculous proposal. With my history, with everything I'd done, I never thought I deserved to be there. I was always worried I'd be found out. As a result, when I did make mistakes, they felt devastating. One time, I went to New York to meet an amazing woman at a cargo airline with whom I had a friendly relationship after having had many meetings together. And, I screwed up. I had to call her up to apologize and tell her that her company would actually have to pay more per month than what we'd agreed and signed upon. The deal ultimately went through, but I beat myself up, thinking, *I don't know what I'm doing. I'm so humiliated, I don't ever want to see her again.* When those kinds of mishaps have occurred in my life, I've just wanted to run away or numb out to escape all those difficult emotions – to escape the feeling of being an imposter.

* * *

I still struggle with imposter syndrome, but I'm more grounded in my self-worth now. In the last few years, I've started leading yoga teacher trainings. They're demanding, and I'm human. I love them and I'm scared of them. I'm always afraid that what I'm offering isn't enough. It's a chunk of money, and I know that there are people who charge a little less. But, I also know there are people who charge a lot more, and I'm glad I'm in the middle. I remember how I felt spending so much money on my first yoga teacher training, so it is important to me to ensure that what I offer is full, rich, and set to a high standard. And, it pays off: the percentage of students who go on to teach after my trainings exceeds eighty percent every year. I want people teaching yoga or teaching something in some way and giving back.

I know people will ask questions that I may not know the answers to. Ana Forrest, one of my teachers, is great at handling this. When people ask her questions she doesn't have the answers to or doesn't have time to answer, she'll say bluntly, "That's not part of this training, let's move on." People often challenge me in my trainings. There are exercises that some people don't like. But, everything I include in my trainings is important; everything is part of the training. Just because someone is not happy with the experience, or they don't like it, doesn't mean I'm going to alter the training to soothe them. That doesn't make sense. I encourage trainees and people in my yoga classes, "Take what you need, leave the rest. But, at least give this a shot. What if you give this a chance, and it's the most freeing experience of your life? I wouldn't want you to miss that."

* * *

While my career was exploding at the bank, I was also part-time counseling at Eighteenth Street Services. If I wasn't traveling, I would come in every couple weeks to talk to guys in the program. The hypocrisy of the situation was that these were the only meetings I was attending. I was telling these guys how to do the work, but I wasn't doing the work myself. There's a saying in the recovery community, "People who don't go to meetings don't find out what happens to people who don't go to meetings." They end up relapsing. I began thinking, *Now that I have all this great information, I can drink like a gentleman for sure.* I rationalized, *If I'm going to close these big deals I should be able to drink. I should be able to have a cigar with my clients. I can manage it.*

By Academy Awards night in 1998, I'd made the decision that I was too young for the sober lifestyle I'd committed to. I shared a bottle of champagne with my neighbor. She passed out after a glass and a half. *Oh, too bad*, I thought, *I'll have to finish that bottle on my own.* I got a little tipsy, but not super drunk. *See?* I thought, *No problem.* I woke up for work the next morning, no hangover, I wasn't craving alcohol. *See? Not a big deal.*

I started telling everyone, "Just so you know, I'm not coming to meetings any more, I'm drinking again." They urged me to come back, but I was resolute: "I actually want to do this right now. This is what I really want to do."

It became a mess quickly on the planes when I was traveling for work. I could get drunk on the company's dime, and none of my friends were there to keep me in check. Once at my hotel, I would also figure out ways to justify ordering wine via room service so I could expense it.

My friends from recovery still wanted to see me, but if I was drinking it was awkward. One time, I showed up an hour late for dinner at a burger joint with two of my sober friends. I was trashed. I will never forget sitting down and seeing the look on my friend Richard's face. "Honey, really?" he shook his head.

"Hah, yeah, it was happy hour," I mumbled, looking down.

"No kidding," he sighed sadly.

Hello – But You'd Never Know It Was Time To Crash Again

In 1999 my career was amazing, sales were skyrocketing, I had a ton of money in the bank, and by August I had bought my house. *See? No problem.* In January of ninety-nine, I met Joe. Joe was – and fifteen years later still is – everything I've ever dreamed of falling in love with and remaining in love with. I refer to him often as my sexy Ken doll. He is beautiful inside and out. His smile and eyes are beyond inviting, and he has a love of adventure. He has a soft demeanor about him that was everything I needed in my life when we met. For so many years now, we are almost always on the same page about everything. Many days, I come home and suggest an outing or an activity, and he replies, "I was thinking the same thing." It doesn't hurt either that cleaning, cooking, and house decorating are therapeutic for him. His family has always welcomed me with open arms and treated me like one of their own. I spent the whole year chasing deals and chasing Joe. We finally had our first real date December sixteenth of 1999.

When I got back from a New Years trip to Bali in mid-January, 2000, Joe and I were inseparable. We were hot and heavy, over at his house, over at my house. We'd spend nights with Honey, our dog, on my carpet in front of the fireplace, talking. I'd begin conversations saying something like, "Listen, I need to tell you some things about me before you hear them from other people..." He never judged me for my past and was always supportive of my tense moments of self-doubt and fear around his friends or in group settings with lots of gay men. Snuggling is one of my most favorite things in the world. As a rule, if I woke up in the middle of the night sweating and needed to roll away from whomever I was sleeping with, that was our last date. With Joe, I couldn't get close enough, night after night.

I knew this relationship was going to shift my everything when I started changing my travel for the bank drastically. I was no longer flying out on Saturdays to arrive places by Sunday to work Monday through Friday and fly home on Saturday. I was flying out on Monday, working Tuesday through Thursday and flying home Thursday nights to get home by Friday. That way I could spend the weekend with Joe. It was easy to hide the alcohol and drugs I was doing because I could do all that on the road. But, after we'd been together for a few months, I sat him down, and said, "I'd like to go out one night."

"What does that mean?" Joe asked.

"I think I'm going to go out and do a little X, maybe do a little K."

"What is that?" he asked, "I've smoked pot, like, once or twice in my life, that's it."

"Huh," I laughed, "You are so not me." I explained that I meant ecstasy and ketamine and told him about what it felt like to take them.

"Okay," he said cautiously, "If it's what you want to do, I guess I'm okay with it."

We went out to this party called Church on a Sunday night. True to my word, I did a little bit of X and K, not too much. It was a challenging night, because of course I wanted to do more than what I had limited myself to, but I was on a mission to keep Joe and to tone down the drug use in my life. To this day, I can remember when the drugs started to wear off, and how miffed I was that I'd promised not to do any more. Thank God there was good music and a sexy man dancing with me. Joe was quiet on the way home. When we got in, I said, "That was fun." He smiled, and nodded. Then I ventured, "Are you okay if I do a little bit more next time?"

"Well, how far is this going to go? Are you going to disappear on me?" he asked, visibly upset, "What's going to happen?"

"I'm going to be right here," I assured him, "It's going to be fine."

Looking back, I can see Joe was hurt that I did not seem to consider him to be a pleasurable enough experience for me. When Joe gets angry, which is rare, his face tenses and he breathes as if he's going to say something, but back then the words didn't come out. Since I used to like to have control of everything, I thought this was great and that I was in the clear.

When he didn't say anything, I added, "You told me it was okay, I don't know why you're pissed at me."

At this time, I was still in heavy-duty salesman mode, and the easiest solution I could see was to sell Joe on a pitch about how much more amazing our time together would be if he tried some drugs. Just a little bit. *Push, push, push.* I used to love projects like this.

The next time I was doing drugs with Joe around, he decided he wanted to try some too. Once he decided to start experimenting, it was on. Joe began traveling with me, and we started to party a bit more. I started to party a lot more, and things got messy for me.

One of the worst parts was, if I didn't use for an hour, in my mind that meant I was okay to drive home. The drugs lasted for hours, so that didn't make any logical sense. One night, Joe and I were driving home on the freeway, and as we approached our exit, I tried to focus on it. I looked at the exit, looked at the freeway, and thought, *Wow, there seem to be extra lane markers. I can't tell which ones are real, and which ones I am hallucinating. I'm going to make a choice here, and it's either going to work out the way I want it to, or it's not.* I'm grateful to be alive to say I chose right, but that could have been it.

For a vacation, Joe, a very good friend, and I went down to Zihuatanejo, Mexico. One evening while we were there, I slurred to our friend, "Do you think I've gone overboard?" He looked me up and down and said, "Honey, we're in Zihuatanejo. The rest of us are shooting fine tequila, and you're drinking a strawberry margarita that is made with strawberry jam. You tell me if you have a problem." I had enough awareness to ask the question, but not quite enough to accept the answer.

Amidst traveling all over the world and signing deals, I was trying my hardest to impress Joe, to convince him to stick around. I went way overboard at Christmas that year. I bought front row tickets to The Nutcracker and future front row tickets to Dolly Parton. Joe still has one of the beads that popped off her outfit in the opening number and rolled off the stage onto the floor. I took him to an extravagant dinner and bought him all sorts of blown glass, which he likes to collect. And clothes. And premium face creams. And more. I think he may have showered me with gifts, too. When I had money, that was my modus operandi when I was uncomfortable. I'd think, *I'll just buy my way through this.* And then if it didn't do the trick, I'd think self-righteously, *How could you not love me, look at what I just did for you.*

When the New Year hit, Joe said, "I don't know if I want to party so much any more." My response: "Sure.

Whatever." He could do what he wanted, that wasn't going to stop me.

Around Easter in 2001, Joe and I went to the White Party down in Palm Springs. The White Party is a gay-boy circuit party that happens all over the world now, with phenomenal international DJs. As if I was there for the music. Most of the people who go are there to do a ton of drugs – at least that's what I always did. It was a three day event, but we were making it four or five. I had forty or fifty hits of ecstasy and ten bottles of ketamine, and the first thing I did when I got down there was call the drug dealer because I was worried I didn't have enough. I barely remember the first night. I kind of remember getting to the party – it had some kind of army fatigues theme – but that's it. The rest of the weekend I was wide awake. Someone couldn't figure out which bottle was K, which bottle was crystal, and which was coke, so they mixed them all together. Joe steered clear of it, but I didn't think twice. It must have shocked my system because on the last night, Sunday, I was taking ecstasy once an hour, and I couldn't get high. *This is going to be crazy*, I thought excitedly, *This is all going to kick in at once. I'm going be ready for this one. This is going to be the mother of all highs.* But, I never got high.

The next morning we were running late for our flight home from the Ontario Airport and we still had to return the rental car. I was in Global Services with United, so I knew I could check in ten minutes before the flight. This was before nine-eleven, so you could still do that. We were speeding along the highway, when I caught a glimpse of a Krispy Kreme sign at the exit just before the airport. I slammed on the brakes, swerved onto the exit at the last moment, and then revved my engine to get away from the car I'd cut off. Joe blinked, gripping the dashboard. "We've gotta go to Krispy Kreme," I said, as if the statement was self-explanatory. When I'd been tweaking and high for days I always craved donuts. After three-to-four-day speed runs in LA, my first meal would be chocolate milk and an apple fritter.

"Are you kidding?" Joe's friend asked from the back seat.

"No, we'll take them on the plane," I laughed, "What flavors do you want?"

We picked up a dozen donuts, and then sped off to the airport. We got to the counter twenty minutes before the flight. The attendant said, "Sorry I can't let you on the flight."

"I'm in Global Services." I said grandiosely, "I have up until ten minutes before the flight."

"Well, I've already put everyone in first class," she protested, diplomatically.

"Doesn't matter." I shrugged, "I know the rules, you have to. I have up until ten minutes before the flight. This is twenty minutes."

She had to downgrade two people, but she got us on the plane. It's moments like that where I see how my grandiosity and insanity fed my shame, which help keep my ego in check today.

When we got in that afternoon, we crawled into bed and didn't wake up until the next morning. I felt terrible, but I had to go to work; I had a conference call regarding a deal I'd been working on for months. The deal was so important that my boss sat in on the call. I was a shaking, shivering, sweating mess. My boss stared at me the whole time. When the call ended, he looked at me and asked, "Uh, are you done with everything you have to do for today?"

"Well, I've gotta check e-mail," I began.

"Do me a favor." he stopped me, "Go home, don't come back the rest of the week, and whatever the hell's going on just get better."

"Okay," I said quietly.

I went home, and crawled into bed. Joe was already in bed. We didn't move the rest of the day. Neither of us. I couldn't feel my fingers, my feet were numb, and there was ringing in my ears. He had the same thing. We both thought we were permanently damaged. Wednesday, same thing. Thursday, same thing.

We were still in bed on Friday watching some TV, and in a commercial break, Oprah came onto the screen: "Coming up at four o'clock, women who drink too much." I said to Joe, "Oh, I love this kind of stuff." We watched the show. One woman told her story about how she and her girlfriends would be out all night and she'd gulp down a margarita an hour. "Wimp!" I scoffed, "Whatever." Toward the end of the show, Oprah had time for only one more guest. The last woman who came on told *my* story. This time, I was silent. I don't know if Joe knew everything that was going on. The woman on Oprah talked about how she would always get home from work and start to drink. She would try to balance out by the time her husband got home, but she would always have a pitcher of something ready for him to start drinking. Once he started getting tipsy, she took it as permission to get trashed. That was my story. I knew the jig was up.

I called my friend Richard, "I think I've gone overboard. I have a problem, I need to come back to recovery."

"Yeah you do," he said, "Just meet me tomorrow for the eleven o'clock meeting."

"Ugh, okay," I said with dread.

"Well actually, meet me at ten o'clock, we'll get a cup of coffee, like the old days."

"Okay," I sighed.

The next day, as we walked into the meeting, I said, "I don't want to introduce myself as a newcomer. I can't believe I'm back here. This is so embarrassing."

"You don't have any memory, do you," Richard interrupted my whining, "This is the meeting where you don't have to introduce yourself. They just say all are welcome."

Lon, my friend who had introduced me to Eighteenth Street Services years earlier, was the secretary. He gave me a piece of literature to read aloud at the end. When it was my time to read, I couldn't. I was crying hysterically. I knew this was going to be hard.

And it was. I tell people all the time, if you're thinking because you're young that you can go out and come back in, let me tell you how hard that first day and year back are, let alone even coming back. In my first couple of months back in recovery someone came up to me at a meeting and said, "Hey, here's the thing you need to know about people who relapse and come back, they don't get a Pink Cloud again. Good luck." That made me furious, but it kept me sober. I thought, *I'll show him.*

I had an abundance of guilt too. For the whole first year, I would go to meetings and then instead of going out with members of that community to process, I would run home and process all this shit with Joe. Shit he didn't understand. When Gay Pride came around, I told Joe, "Listen, if I say we're going out tonight, that means out. You know what I'm talking about." It meant I was going to relapse. "I just can't promise that I can keep this together. I just don't know. I don't know if I'm going to make it, Joey." Joe used to ask me how I was doing all the time. Finally, I said, "Please don't ask me that every day. The answer's not on a day-to-day level, it changes moment-to-moment."

Those first couple months of sobriety were so hard, I felt so unstable. I'd think, *I've only got three days, what's the big deal, I can get three days again.* In reality, you never know, that one "last" time you drink or use could be the time you hurt someone, or overdose, or drive your car off a bridge.

Joe and I got outside help too. When we started going to counseling, I thought, *I've messed up again. Here's the most amazing guy I've ever met in my life* – probably, anyway, I never stuck around for the other ones – *and I have once again messed it up.* It never occurred to me that we were doing the counseling to stay together. Never. I don't think he had much hope for us either. We both wanted to at least break up with a little dignity and grace, and without harming and hurting each other. We wanted to have a loving transition. I knew how to do the opposite. I'd abandoned my mom and my sister, and then run away from my dad, too. Not only had I done the same thing to Bob, I'd trashed his place in the process. I had walked out on Kevin and so many others like him, blatantly leaving them for prostitution and drugs.

Sauca

When people pick lint off their yoga mat or sweep their foot across the mat when stepping forward, I say, "You should have cleaned your mat before you got here, don't sweep the mat. Practice *sauca*, cleanliness and purity." *Sauca* is not only about having a clean mat, it's about a clean way of moving the body – with focus and concentration, with precision. It's about a clean way of being.

When I was out there drinking and using, I had neither cleanliness nor purity. I used to have disgusting two-, three-, four-, or five-day stays at the bathhouse or at the Crystal Sandy Hotel. I had no change of clothes, and sometimes I wouldn't even bother showering from trick to trick to trick.

Some people show up to yoga in a way that reminds me of how I used to present myself. Some students leave a puddle of sweat behind without a second thought about wiping it up. Some students wear the same yoga clothes day after day. I no longer smoke and I *neti* (a yoga practice for cleansing the sinuses) frequently, so I have a good sense of smell: I know when someone has sweat all over their YogiToes mat towel, rolls it up with the mat after class, sticks it somewhere to fester overnight, and then rolls it back out the next day for class. Stinky.

Just like all the other *yamas* and *niyamas*, the habit of *sauca* or the violation of *sauca* is never isolated to one aspect of our lives, it will seep into all areas. When I was constantly allowing men to use my body in ways that were in blatant violation of what I wanted or needed – ways that were impure – it's no wonder that I had no problem filling my body with substances – more impurities – that kept me out of touch with my misery. When the sales I made for the bank felt dirty, it's no wonder I had a hard time staying clean. We cultivate what we practice.

My first step toward *sauca* was to get clean and sober. Since that's been established, I've been able to refine my practice of purity and cleanliness in other aspects of life. Now, I have awareness around cleanliness, honoring others' experience of my body. If possible, I wash at least my face and hands, and change clothes every time I teach so I'm not carrying students' sweat, odors, and energetic baggage from one class to another.

Cleanliness and purity also pertain to the other things we put in our bodies too. Instead of mindlessly gorging nearly 3000 calories in a single sitting at Burger King, I am clean in what I eat, in that I choose foods that nourish me. When I have my oatmeal, Greek yogurt, cinnamon, and cardamom in the morning, I am aware that it is nourishing me physically, giving me the energy I need for the day ahead. When I go out to Mitchell's Ice Cream for a single scoop (or sometimes double), I know that I am nourishing my spirit and soul. When I eat, I am connected to exactly what the gift is that I'm getting from my food.

A high ratio of trainees enter my teacher training vegetarian, vegan, or raw, and leave eating fish and chicken. It's not because I tell them they should. I ask, "Do you *know* that works for you? Or, did you just read somewhere, or did someone tell you, 'If you practice yoga you should definitely not be eating meat, you shouldn't eat ice cream, you shouldn't have caffeine.' Who told you that's right or wrong? Did you buy into something without investigating what's good for your body?" Unfortunately, with all the amazing and well-meaning efforts to promote sustainability, there are so many different messages out there about how to eat clean, that our path can become unclear, and our actions become messy and out-of-focus. Ignoring our experience and following rigid guidelines is another form of mindless eating.

When it comes to thoughts, purity comes back to *satya*, truthfulness. I have to be honest about what my thoughts are. This morning when a scooter cut my car off while I was driving, my first thought was *dumb-ass*. Even though my initial thought wasn't very nice, the act of *sauca* is to be aware of it rather than trying to pretend I'm too yogic to even think such a thing. The act of *metta*, loving kindness, is asking, *Is it timely? Is it necessary?* I didn't need to roll down the window of my car and aggressively voice my thought. It wouldn't have changed anything.

Now that I'm able to acknowledge my pure thoughts, if you ask me a question, you can rely on me telling the truth. When I was on drugs, I was unreliable. Now, if I say I can, I will. There is purity about my relationships, friendships, and in my intentions with other people. In the past, I've come from a place of self-centered fear, and I've overcompensated for that by obsessing about whether my actions will hurt others. Now I don't worry about that as much. I've practiced *sauca* for long enough that I've developed it as a habit and I trust my intuition.

When it is time for action, I need to fuel my actions in a way that is clean: in a way that's consistent with what's important to me. I ask myself, *What are my visions and goals? What am I fueling? How am I fueling it?* Some people fuel action with anger, resentment, jealousy, and revenge. To me, that's not an appropriate fuel anymore. *Am I fueling in a way that's not being a hypocrite? Am I practicing what I'm teaching and preaching?*

Les Leventhal

PART IX: TAPAS

Do you have the discipline to give away physical possessions you no longer need? Are there thought patterns you repeat that served you once, but are now self-destructive? Which features of your identity that no longer serve you can you find the courage to let go of?

Yoga 101

I started doing yoga in 1999, a couple years before I got clean again. It was just exercise then, just a form of stretching. I was lifting weights and doing aerobics. I had injuries from all that, and someone suggested I try yoga. My first class was with Steph Snyder at Gold's Gym. She's one of the most popular teachers in San Francisco today, but back then she was brand new. She taught the type of class you wouldn't normally see at a gym. We held horse stance, a wide leg squat, forever to do *uddhiyanna bandha*, drawing the belly in so far that the rib cage protrudes, and *nauli*, making a circular movement with the abdominal muscles to massage the digestive organs. Afterward, I thought, *What was that? That was crazy.* But, my curiosity was piqued, so I tried another class. I continued going to a class here and there, and slowly I started practicing more and more.

When I got sober in 2001, I started doing a bit more yoga, and by 2002 I was doing a lot more. I started to listen to more than just the exercise parts. I still had the remnants of LA syndrome: *If I look flawless, then you'll love me.* As I practiced yoga, the critical voices from the pornography industry and from the people who had been disgusted by my life choices were replaced with voices of some of my yoga teachers who kept saying that my body was okay just the way it was. That *I* was okay just the way I was. Some of the teachers who got to know me also started challenging me to look at what I was doing for work and ask myself why I was doing it. They encouraged me to ask myself why I was chasing money. Was money really the path to happiness? When I spent all my time and energy chasing money, chasing deals, and then came home at the end of the day, what was left for my loved ones? Was this what I wanted? *What am I doing at my job?* I wondered. If you took away the business suit and the brief case, my job – or how I was working it, anyway – sounded a whole lot like prostitution. I was sacrificing what mattered most to me to make more, more, more money.

Much to my surprise, counseling with Joe was going well. I started hearing concepts in yoga like, *asteya*, non-stealing. *Is all the travel I'm doing enhancing my relationship or taking away from it? Stealing from it?* I began to ask myself. I always flew on weekends. I would leave on Friday or Saturday to get somewhere by Sunday, so I could work all week, and fly home the next weekend. Once I realized the affect this was having on my relationship, my business trips got shorter and shorter. My boss thought such quick trips to different continents were crazy, but he couldn't argue, because I was still getting the job done.

I started attending classes with Howard Tom at Gold's. I used to complain to him that I wasn't getting any more flexible. He said to me, "You know, if you want to get more flexible, maybe don't have the double espresso on your way to the gym, then lift weights for an hour, then come to class. Have a juice and just come to class, skip the weights." He would repeat the message to me every class, "Are you getting more flexible? Are you seeking more flexibility in your life?" I started to realize he wasn't only talking about my physical body.

I'd been going to classes a while, and then I discovered workshops. *Wow*, I thought, *there's more than just this class stuff, there's a whole other world here.* A deeper practice of yoga is what got me thinking, *My recovery comes first.* I get to do everything I'm doing because I am clean and sober. If I don't stay clean and sober, everything else is out the door. But, the yoga community isn't a replacement for the recovery community. Sometimes I'd do a whole weekend of yoga workshops, instead of going to meetings. Yoga's so spiritual I thought it would be okay. I was also traveling frequently, and not going to meetings on the road.

One weekend, I went into a meeting at seven in the morning and whined about how hard it was to attend these meetings, about how busy I was, about all the other hardships of my life. A guy walked up to me and said clearly and simply, "Your life is a mess, and you're going to drink and use again. That means you want to die. I bet you have plans tonight. Cancel them, be at my house at seven p.m., I can help you." I never had anyone speak to me like that before in my life.

I went to his house, and he ended up being my sponsor for six years. The first thing he said was, "If you don't quit this job, it will kill you. Either the job will kill you 'cause you'll drink and use again or it will kill you from the stress and anxiety, and the pressure that you, your bosses, and the whole bank put you under." Deep down, I knew this was true. I had to leave my job. Just like I was an expert at leaving men abruptly and callously, I'd quit many of my jobs by exploding at my supervisor, slamming something down on their desk, and storming out the door. My sponsor-to-be interrupted my unpleasant fantasy about how I'd have to quit my job at the bank: "You can't just walk in tomorrow and quit, though." We went onto discuss how I could make this transition with care and compassion for myself and for others. Just as in yoga there were intermediate steps on the way to *hanumanasana*, full splits, there was a process here too. I finally started to learn how to do things slowly.

It took me about eighteen months to figure out my finances enough to quit the job. But my boss knew. He came to my office one day and said, "You're going to quit aren't you."

"Huh?" I said, feigning innocence.

"Well, I know your pension vests in six or eight months, so I assume you're waiting around for that."

I started laughing, I'm not good at lying.

"I'm not going to can you." he said, "It's going to suck that you're not going to be around. You've been my top salesman for years. It sucks to lose someone like you. But I get that this job burns people out. The only thing that bothers me is that you're going to beat me out the door.

And I'm jealous." I laughed much less nervously than before. He continued, "And I get that other things are happening in your life."

The day I quit, we were up in Guerneville, Russian River for the weekend. My boss lived nearby in Novato. I called him up and said, "We're going to stop by on the way home," but I didn't tell him what it was about. When I got there, he said, "Either you're going to tell me that you and Joe are adopting kids or that you're quitting."

"I'm quitting." I said decisively, "I can quit at work tomorrow, if that's how you want me to do it, but I'm quitting." As those words came out of my mouth, I felt liberated and terrified all at the same time.

He understood. The president of the company didn't. When he found out I was quitting he asked, "What are you doing instead?"

"I'm not doing anything, I'm just quitting," I said.

"Well, where are you going to work?" He wasn't getting it.

"I'm not. I just quit. I'm protecting my life. I don't want to die." That was a huge revelation and transition for me. *I want to have a life.* I took a huge leap of faith and trust in myself, my friendships that I had at the time, and in Joe. I had faith that whatever was about to unfold it was going to be okay.

Life After Bankasana

When I quit my job, I had what I would have liked to think was plenty of money in the bank to maintain my standard of living for two years. I had had quite the high lifestyle. I'd spent seventy-five percent of my time on the road, where everything was paid for, so I was used to living on an expense account. I liked to eat out, and I'd never thought about where I was eating or how I was eating. It didn't matter if I went out for a $100 sushi dinner three nights in a row. The first Friday I didn't get a paycheck I panicked, "The number in my bank account had gone down. It's gone down and it's not going to go back up. It's just going to keep going down, down, down." The more money I'd earned, the less I was able to let any of it go, and that attachment to my wealth was amplified now that I was out of work. From the day I quit, I still have $28.31 in a savings account I opened many years ago. I don't know why I keep it. Maybe because it reminds me of the twenty-eight dollars I had in my pocket when I arrived LA twenty-eight years ago.

"Two years," Joe said, "You can't even go two weeks? You've got two years ahead of you. A year and fifty more weeks."

"Oh God," I said, the harsh reality of my decision setting in, "Ahh, I'm in trouble."

I was supposed to relax, take a year off, and let some of that time be about nothing. That didn't happen. I immediately started looking at yoga teacher trainings. A few people had suggested I do one. I didn't think I wanted to teach, but I thought a month of yoga with a master teacher somewhere away from my life could be fun and keep me out of trouble.

I'd taken classes with Baron Baptiste, Rodney Yee, Richard Freedman, Shiva Rea, and Ana Forrest at the Yoga Journal Conference. The one who spoke to the animalistic aggressive salesman in me was Ana. The rest were too loving at the time. Ana has a crazy past filled with all the unimaginable things that happen to children, and she has healed that trauma through yoga. She's all about brazenly taking the power back from our abusers. Her sweaty classes are all about long holds, defying gravity, tons of core work, and doing things we shouldn't be able to do. She challenges her students to go to places that are challenging, terrifying, or uncomfortable so that we can face our fears. So that we can finally release our trauma. I still had the personality of a ruthless salesperson, who would think aggressively, *You want what I'm selling, I will show you how this is going to benefit you.* Ana said the same thing, "I will show you how this yoga is going to benefit you," in a raw, factual way that I immediately connected with.

Even so, I dragged my feet the whole way. I sent in the application without the required deposit. Someone e-mailed me to say they needed my deposit.

I replied, "I'm out of work right now, but it's coming, I promise." The words I said were true, but I was a total liar, purposely misleading the person on the other end of the line. Sure, I was out of work, but with six digits in cash sitting in my checking account.

Before the training, Ana came to San Francisco to lead some workshops at Yoga Tree. When I'd done the workshop with her at the Yoga Journal Conference, I hadn't introduced myself, so I assumed I would be anonymous.

When I got to Yoga Tree Castro around quarter to eight for Ana's Friday evening heart openers workshop, the place was packed. Ana walked in with her long hair all braided up, and people immediately flocked around her. Ana embodies Native American ceremonial ancestry. When I look at her, I can see the dirt and grit from her childhood, but even the first time I saw her, I immediately knew she had also done the necessary cleansing to be where she is in her life. She has a voice that says in tone alone, *Seriously? You're going to bail from dolphin pose that fast? Why did you even bother coming?*

After greeting some of the other students, Ana looked around and her eyes locked on me. She walked right up to me, and said, "So, you're Les, right?"

"Yeah," I said, eyes wide.

"We have your application for teacher training. Maybe you don't know this, but we have a waiting list," she enunciated, tracing the shape of a list with her hands, "By the end of the weekend, if I haven't gotten at least a deposit from you, we're yanking you from the training."

In my first heart opener, I thought, *Fuck you, Ana*, but I stuck around and threw myself into the workshop anyway. By ten o'clock at night we were doing *urdhva dhanurasana*, full wheel, a deep stimulating backbend, and I was totally immersed. After that workshop, I didn't sleep, I felt like I was high on drugs. I loved it. Some people would say "blissed out." Whatever. I felt like I was tweaking. But not in a way that felt dangerous, or like I shouldn't be driving. Rather than feeling numbed out, I felt deeply connected and vibrantly alive.

Still on that high, when I went to her workshop the next morning, I thought, *This is great.* My eyes were bugging out, and someone asked, "Are you okay?"

"Yeah," I said, "I didn't sleep well last night."

"I heard a lot of people say they didn't sleep."

After the Saturday afternoon workshop, a bunch of us went to dinner at Thai House. The owner, Kitty, now comes to my yoga classes. Having barely eaten anything all day, when I sat down, I thought, *I have to eat.* I ordered a ton of food. But, after only eating a small portion of what was set in front of me, I was aware that I was full. I didn't need any more. No one had to say anything about food. No one had to explicitly teach me that lesson about moderation and quantity. On its own, the yoga shifted my awareness in such a way that my nutrition was altered.

That night I went home and still wasn't feeling tired, so I decided to shave. When I went to trim my eyebrows, I forgot to put the comb on, and I trimmed the first one off completely. I saw my reflection in the mirror and yelped. Joe came running in to see me gawking at myself in the mirror, took one look at my reflection, and burst out laughing, "What are you going to do now?" he said wiping away tears.

"Well," I said, "my options are to trim the second one and then paste the trimmings over where the first one was. Or, just shave off the second one entirely to match."

I walked into the morning workshop on Sunday with both eyebrows trimmed off. When I ran into Carrie, Yoga Tree's manager at the time, she nearly fell down laughing, "What happened to you?" she howled, "You look like this," she said, widening her eyes and raising her eyebrows all the way up, "But, with no eyebrows."

Eyebrowless, I walked up to Ana Forrest, gave my check over, and said, "I'll see you at the training."

"You know it's going to be good for you," she said, "You're just ready for this, I can tell."

I knew she was right. Part of my hesitance came from a sense of unfamiliarity. It had been ages since I had done something for myself like this. Another contributing factor was fear. I knew the training would be demanding, and I knew other people would say and do things in the training that would be uncomfortable for me to experience. There would be people who would offer me reflection of who I'd been or who I still was – that can be hard to see, even today. Also, it felt like I was going to take time away from my relationship with Joe. It never occurred to me that the training would be fantastic for our relationship, which it turned out to be in so many ways. This yoga journey has been the most amazing thing in my entire life, and I almost missed it all. I hope that when I die, angels come show me a review of my life including all the forks in the road, and how my choices affected the people around me and the world at large.

As the training approached, I started to get cranky, thinking about all the money I'd have to spend on accommodations and food. My only solace was that I was driving down in my big fancy Mercedes.

On the first day of the training, Ana didn't hold back; the yoga was intense. In the afternoon we began with a check-in. Sitting in a circle, each person had three minutes to introduce themselves. When it came around to my turn I looked around at the room full of women, many of whom reminded me of my mom or my sister. Without hiding my irritation, I ranted about how I was out of work. I complained that I'd already calculated that this month in LA was going to cost me six or seven thousand dollars. I expressed my bitterness at how, in her introduction, Ana had told us we should plan to get all sorts of body work and therapy done during the training, which would make my month even more expensive. In conclusion, I said, "So, I'm here to suck up, soak up, and steal every bit of information I possibly can, in case I want to teach."

Unfazed by my forwardness, Ana looked at me in a way that only Ana can. She lowered her chin slightly, raised one eyebrow, and quirked one side of her mouth down – it's a sort of encouraging look that communicates, *We have work to do together and we will get it done. Just trust me.* She said, "Next time you talk for three minutes, it's advisable to take at least one breath." For once, I didn't have a comeback. I passed the talking stick onto the next person. Ana's talking stick is a part of her Native American ceremony for talking circles. It has a crystal at one end that you hold near your heart and is made with feathers that she has collected out in the wild. I use talking sticks now for my circles in teacher trainings too. It gets people focused and honest in the first breath, with the very first word.

Although I started the day with some resistance, by the end of the first day I felt great. I loved what we had done and how we had done it. The training started on a Friday, and by Monday we found out we'd be teaching a class to the public the following weekend. Ana split the group in two. My group would co-teach a class that Friday night until ten at night, and then we'd have to stick around until eleven or eleven-thirty for a video review. The other group would be teaching the following afternoon. Someone from my group asked, "Since we'll have to stay extra time Friday night, does that mean we can skip the practice in the morning?" No, it did not.

The class we taught was amazing, and the video review was hysterical. I had the best experience. I was, of course, happy it was over, but it had been fantastic to teach. I wasn't expecting that. I expected it to suck. I expected the students to have a terrible experience. During the next morning's practice, I was paying attention to the class, but also reliving the previous night. It had been so amazing. The next week, we got different pieces to teach, refined our teaching technique, worked with different partners, and practiced teaching with big groups and small groups. When it came time to teach the public again, I wasn't fearful or plagued with self-doubt as I had been the previous week. I was thinking, *I'm so excited about this!* After that, I began asking myself, *Do I really want to teach?* By the end of the training that spark would grow into a bonfire.

It was as if I moved down through the *chakras,* the energy centers traditionally thought to lie along the spine: I had a thought (crown *chakra*). Then I had a vision (third eye *chakra*), to teach yoga. Then I started giving it some words (throat *chakra*), admitting it to myself. Then I started talking to Joe, which for me is the heart (heart *chakra*). And then giving it some fire (solar plexus *chakra*), allowing myself to get invested in it and to get excited about it. Then getting down into the survival: *Is this sustainable? Can I support this life?* (sacral *chakra*). And then that whole thing manifested for me (root *chakra*). I saw how it could happen, and I knew how to get there. I knew resources I needed, and I knew lots of people teaching at lots of studios. Even before the end of the training, I was ready. I didn't even want to do the anatomy part, I wanted to get home and start teaching.

Getting In As A Yoga Teacher At Yoga Tree

I graduated from my yoga teacher training on a Thursday. On the drive home from Los Angeles, I called Carrie at Yoga Tree. "What is going on?" I said.

"How are *you?*" she replied, knowing that I'd just completed my teacher training with Ana.

"Oh my God. Amazing. I'm ready to teach."

"Yeah, I'll bet," she said.

"No," I emphasized, "I'm ready to teach. I want to teach at Yoga Tree."

She laughed, "Everyone comes out of yoga trainings, and they want to teach at Yoga Tree. There's not room for everybody. People go out and they teach at gyms and other studios first and then come back with more experience."

"Well, okay," I sighed, then said conversationally, "So how have things been at Yoga Tree while I've been gone?"

"There's a lot of craziness," she said, "Jamie left and we haven't secured a regular teacher for the six a.m. classes, and no one's showing up to sub. We're kind of going nuts about that."

"I'll teach the six a.m. classes," I said quickly, "I'm up at, like, five."

"They're not going to let you teach," she said sympathetically.

"But no one's showing up. What are they going to do? Get rid of those classes? Call Tara and Tim," (the owners at Yoga Tree), "and tell them that I'm willing, and then call me back and let me know what they say." I was still a total salesman.

We hung up, and then an hour later she called me back, "Tomorrow, Friday, you're going to teach us a class. It's going to be me, bring Joe, tell him to bring a friend, and I'll bring someone else who works here who would be a good evaluator."

"Okay great," I exclaimed.

That night I taught a practice one-on-one class to my yoga teacher friend, to get some feedback. The next day, I went to Yoga Tree and taught the audition class to four people. The woman Carrie brought to evaluate me said, "You're green, you're new, but it was a pretty good class. You maintained control and you were able to teach to all four of us, and we were all different levels."

Carrie called Tim and Tara, and the very next Monday, five days after I finished my teacher training I started subbing the six a.m. classes, Monday through Friday. After my first class, I felt so good that I called Tara and asked her if I could sub any other classes as well. She was hesitant because I was such a new teacher, but Yoga Tree was short on subs at the time, so she reluctantly agreed.

"Excellent," I replied, and encouraged by her concession, I ventured, "By the way, these classes at six a.m., I don't want to be a sub, I want to be the regular teacher on the schedule."

"We'll see," she said cautiously.

Within a few weeks, I was subbing tons of classes, teaching three or four classes a day, every day. They finally did give me those six a.m. classes, and I built them up to fifteen or twenty people, which was more than they were getting at nine a.m. After a few months, I caught wind that Yoga Tree was looking for a new teacher for a potential popular Saturday slot. Without hesitation, I told Tara and the other Yoga Tree managers, "I want that class." There were other contenders, but I had proven I could build a class, and the yoga business in San Francisco is some parts about yoga seniority, and some parts about the numbers. So, they ended up giving it to me. Back then at Yoga Tree, a small class was forty or fifty. The most popular teachers were pulling 100 or 120. The Saturday class I picked up was barely getting double digits at the time due to lots of subs, and the Yoga Tree managers said they wanted it at thirty students by the end of the year and forty by June. The salesman inside of me finds numbers deliciously irresistible. My desire to succeed was alive, and the fire was burning hot.

By the end of the year I had forty or fifty. By that following June, seventy or eighty. When classes started rocking out for me, other opportunities came my way. I told Yoga Tree I couldn't keep doing six a.m.'s every day, and that I wanted some other classes in better time slots. As my schedule shifted and changed, all my classes started building even more, and it wasn't long until I was one of Yoga Tree's most popular teachers. I learned that I had more to offer my students when I taught fewer classes per day and gave myself a day off. After a couple years, I began offering workshops – local and afar – then yoga retreats, then yoga teacher trainings. Even now, I sometimes have the same thought that I did the first time I taught in Ana Forrest's training, *Wow, I love teaching yoga.*

As I've matured as a teacher, an amazing transformation has been to let go of needing packed classes to teach well and to feel satisfied. All I want to do is share this crazy thing called yoga in the same way this gift was given to me. Trusting that it is more sustainable to focus on my purpose than to get caught up in numbers has allowed my teaching to be wildly authentic. In class, I share my experiences, hopes, and the once-dormant dreams that yoga can wake up for us all. As a result, I have met people who offer perspective on my experience; support, fuel, and even fulfill my hopes; and breathe life into my dreams.

Tapas

When I worked at the bank, I loved driving my Mercedes. I got it in February of 1999. I had just got a big fat commission check, and I thought to myself, *I am buying myself a pretty-shiny.* I went with a friend to the

Mercedes dealer, and pointed to a slate gray car, "I want that color."

"That one is $50,000," (or something ridiculous like that) the salesman said. "But," he continued gesturing toward two black cars and a red one, "we have these three over here. Everything's the same except no heated seats. You can have any of them for $28,000."

My friend pulled me aside and whispered excitedly, "Take it! They're offering you $20,000 off. Heated seats only add $1,000. They're just trying to move these because it's the last day of the month. You'll love it; black is great."

"No," I whined, "I want the slate gray. I want sexy." So, I bought the more expensive car, and proudly paid for the whole thing upfront.

I loved driving it. It was so luxurious, so comfortable; it had those heated seats. I probably could have had it upgraded to wipe my ass if I'd wanted it to. In my life now, I'd be lying if I said I didn't miss it some days. But, when I started teaching yoga it felt weird to drive a big fat Mercedes to class. Within six months, I knew I had to get rid of my car. I felt fraudulent driving it. I felt like it isolated me from others. A big part of buying a status symbol car for me was to send the message, "I'm different from the rest of you." I feel right in the little

Honda Civic that I drive around San Francisco. It has a few dents and paint chips. I have humbly arrived at a place in my life where my message is, "I'm just the same as you and anyone else in the world." I'm not wasting the resources of the universe as much.

The experience with my car spurred me to examine other aspects of my life to consider how I could practice *tapas*, austerity, living with less. I looked at what I was consuming, what I was eating, what I was wearing, where I was shopping. I had come from a place of overindulgence. I had big Kenneth Cole and Duty Free habits since I used to get stuck at airports all the time – shoes, jackets and face creams were my thing. People knew me because I used to show up to the yoga studio all the time in suits. At the Intercontinental Hotel that I always stayed at in Chicago when I worked for the bank, there was a Kenneth Cole store right across the street, and I'd usually come home with a pair of shoes or a couple of jackets. One time Joe said, "You don't even wear some of these shoes, not even once a year when we go to the ballet. What's the point?" I didn't have a good reason. It was just an effect of my insatiable desire for more, more, more.

Now, I buy a pair of tennis shoes every couple of years – whenever the last pair falls apart. I just bought a new computer because the one I had for thirteen years finally died, but I didn't buy a printer, scanner, and all the other accessories the salespeople tried to up-sell me on. Joe and I can share. When I'm thinking of buying something now, I ask myself, *Do I need this? Is it necessary? What do I need to sustain my life?* I have come to realize I don't need something shiny and new every month or every year.

I live with less food. If a meal I order at a restaurant is a big portion, I don't have to finish it all right now. I can save it to enjoy over the next couple days. That wasn't an option for me before.

The practice of austerity can apply to the physical practice as well. I don't have to do a hardcore *vinyasa* practice six days a week any more. It doesn't always have to be a crazy sweatfest, intense, on-the-edge, dive-in-with-my-guts-and-get-aggressive marathon session. Ceremony can be soft, light, and short. In the movie *Steel Magnolias*, Julia Roberts' character isn't supposed to get pregnant because of her diabetes, but she decides to have a baby anyway. One of her lines is, "I'd rather have fifteen minutes of something wonderful than a lifetime of nothing at all." In that vein, I'd rather have ten minutes of complete solitude and silence to meditate than an hour of sitting still with the TV on in the background and the dogs vying for my attention, and checking e-mail on my mobile device every time I hear a notification.

PART X: SVADHYAYA

Do you like spending time with yourself enough to take time out of your day for solitude and self-study? What is out of balance in your life and what is in harmony? Which daily practices allow you to develop love and compassion for yourself and others?

To Master, Teach

Some of the students who practice with me ask, "Are you always happy and joyful?" I respond, "You only see me when I'm teaching yoga. You only see me when I'm deeply connected to my passion." After years of work in yoga and recovery, I've finally started to drift away from that aggressive salesperson who bullied his way into a teaching position at the top studio in San Francisco, away from the addict who taught five classes a day, and away from the prostitute who would do anything to please people. But, I still have challenges. I still have desire and temptation.

When I first got sober sometimes the only safe part of my day was the hour I was in a meeting. Some days I would go to two or three meetings, especially on the weekends, just so I wouldn't have any free time. Teaching also sometimes provides that band-aid for me. It's an hour and a half that I'm not connected to anyone or anything except for the people there. It's a gift of presence.

My recovery is also greatly supported by yoga. When I'm facing challenge or questioning, I turn to my practice. *Asana*, practicing the poses, is a huge part of my meditation – answers come on the mat. Answers also come in seated meditation. They come in my prayers too.

If I had cancer, I wouldn't just go get chemo. I'd investigate a whole array of other healing to support me through the process. It's important to have my practices of recovery, yoga, and meditation. It's important for me to have my communities. I tell my classes, "Your mind can be a dangerous neighborhood, don't go there alone." I have a disease called stinkin' thinkin' and sometimes I can swing from happiness to anger, to fear, to imposter syndrome, to saying "everything's great" when everything isn't great. All the practices I do act as band-aids and medicines that support me and remind me that it's okay to feel like that. I have a committee upstairs sitting at the boardroom table, constantly analyzing my situation, and telling me it's not okay to be experiencing what I am. Because of this, I constantly have to remind myself that it's okay not to have all the answers, it's okay to be confused, it's okay to be seeking.

I've learned that the finding is in the seeking. When I ask myself questions, they are often their own answers. That the question came up for me has unearthed something; maybe that there is a problem in my life. Sometimes the solution is just that recognition. Sometimes, the solution is to keep going back to the source, to revisit that thing that brought up the question in the first place. When students come to me hoping for answers, often my advice is, "Whatever it is you're doing that is bringing up questions, whatever is allowing you to continue to find, keep doing it. Keep going." Even if you're prostituting, there's a finding there, and there will be a knowing there when the unconscious becomes conscious.

I taught my Yoga and Recovery workshop in Dallas, and when I walked out to get some food afterward, there was a woman outside the hotel smoking a cigarette. I could tell by the way she was sitting that she was drunk. "Hi Leeesssss," she said.

"Hi, it's great to see you," I said, assuming she must have practiced with me before.

"You haven't met me before," she said, "but I definitely should have come to your recovery workshop today."

"Maybe," I laughed, and then added, "I'll do it again sometime."

It's not my place to tell people what I think they've got going on in their lives. If people are questioning, I say, "Keep questioning, keep investigating, see what's going on."

Svadhyaya

Svadhyaya is the study of the self, my favorite of all the *niyamas*. When I relapsed and was back out drinking and using, my ethics were of convenience; if it fit me, if it benefited me, it was ethical. It was through studying myself that I was able to change that. Yoga pushed me back into recovery. It was that self-reflection on the mat that made me think: *What am I doing? I was clean for five years. That wasn't a mistake.*

The only reason we study the self is because we have an intuition that change is needed. To get in touch, we have to have been out of touch. In meditation, I ask myself, *Am I just telling people to go out and help others, or am I actually going out to help others?* A practice of *svadhyaya* will bring awareness to areas of hypocrisy in our lives.

I practice with teachers who I love; the ones that take me right to those places I want to be, which are sometimes challenging, sometimes super fun and enjoyable. These teachers will take me to places I don't want to look at. They make it safe for me to explore the shadow sides of myself; I get to see that I can be impatient and crispy. I get to be reminded that I'm an addict of many things, and I'm in recovery and seek love and acceptance. All of that is part of me, and that's okay. Sometimes the work is not to change anything, it's to accept myself and others as we are. My teachers won't give me a pose or sequence that will eliminate impatience from my life, or produce only patience. They allow me to experience my impatience so that I may come into acceptance of it. If you come to my classes in a state of sadness or grief, my class won't necessarily move you beyond that – it will hopefully allow you to experience that sadness and grief for however long that's supposed to be in your life.

I also practice with teachers that make me think, *Ugh, I can only do this once a month, because otherwise I'll pull out the hair that's growing in my ears.* (At least I've got some there.) *This makes every part of my spirit and belly flip and turn and curdle like bad cream.* However, I often say to my own students, "You don't like this posture? Try it again anyway. If this was a science experiment you'd never just do one trial. Confirm you don't like it." It's the same idea with the teachers whose classes I don't love. You never know, maybe the teacher is working on some of the same stuff I am, and one day everything will change: they'll be able to guide me and show me something no other teacher can. Or, maybe something will shift in me so that I'll need exactly what they have to offer. Similarly, for the people reading this book who think, *This isn't me, addiction isn't a part of my life,* don't throw the book away, that could change. Today's gift can become tomorrow's challenge and today's challenge can become tomorrow's gift.

If I had enough time, every class I taught would be a crazy over-the-top experience that takes people apart and puts them back together again – sometimes ninety minutes isn't enough and I have to save that for retreats and trainings. I don't teach classes in which you'll be comfortable the whole time: I hope you shake, I hope you fall. I want you to have those experiences in yoga so you can observe yourself in them instead of getting caught up in them. When people have breakdowns, I'm there, I can listen, I can reflect back and not have to fix them. It's not my place to tell people who or how they should be. That's something they have to evaluate and investigate for themselves.

We'll never discover everything about ourselves, because we're always changing. Every year, every day, every minute. With day-to-day changes in my body, my practice is different. It changes with injuries too. As I get older, what's important to me changes. When I was in Houston recently, I was giving instructions, and suddenly a few students looked up and said, "What?"

I said, "Did I just say: step your foot to the front of your mat, turn the toes to ten o'clock, and open onto the outer edge of your foot, or was that just in my head?"

"We didn't hear a thing," one person laughed. Maybe I'm not as sharp and focused as I used to be. I get to study that part of myself too.

A large component of my *svadhyaya* is what I want to teach people and how I want to be with my students. The most important thing is that I'm living what I'm teaching. When I am expressing myself straight from my heart, informed by my experiences, it allows me to be my most authentic self.

It's Time

There are some things I would have loved to change along the way, but if I did, I don't know if I'd be where I am right now, and I love where I am right now. It's not without its challenges, but I'm grateful for those, too. Even in the face of these challenges, rather than carelessly making choices, I now have the self-control and awareness to use the *yamas* and *niyamas* to guide my action. I ask myself, *Is it useful, is it necessary, is it truthful? Is it selfish, is it fear-based, is it retaliation-based?* Before coming into a place where I could live ethically and relate to others in a responsible way, I had to lose myself in a big way. I needed to take every drink, every snort, every line, every pill. I needed to tell every lie. I needed to steal all the money and jewelry. I needed to screw everyone I screwed, physically and mentally.

When there's addiction involved, you never quite know where you are until you're able to see it in hindsight. It's okay. You're going to do whatever you want to do. When I was in the thick of it, there was no one who could tell me otherwise. I wouldn't have listened had anyone said, "You have a problem, you need to stop." I needed to find that myself. That's the thing about addiction: we can be faced with the most amazing evidence for why not to do something, but hours later there we are doing it again anyway. It wouldn't have helped to throw money at my problem, send me on a vacation, or send me to rehab. Before I was ready to change, no one could help me, other than to say, "I'm here if you need to talk. If you ever decide you want to change, I can help you," or maybe, "If you give me a few minutes, I can tell you about what this led to for me, about how it affected my choices and my relationships, and about some of the work I had to do because of it."

There are people out there drinking, using, prostituting, and in and out of jail. There's another way to life. There are options. People can change their lifestyle at any time, at any age. But, it takes work. They have to come to a place where they're ready to do the work.

When you fall into prostitution, you get so dissociated from your body that you don't feel like you're working. You tell yourself that you're playing and partying. I got to drink, do a lot of drugs, get treated to nice dinners, fly to different cities for gigs. I got paid lots of cash and got to steal jewelry on top of that. It was fun for a while, but at some point you wake up and think, *How did this happen? Who did this to me? How did I get here?* It took me years to recognize I was responsible for how low things got in my life. Even when I first got clean, I held a lot of blame for other people. When I relapsed, they weren't there to blame any more. I recognized it was me.

It's not easy to let people go through their process. We know that some people have tragic things happen to them. Some people die, some people go to jail or to other institutions. Some of the people in jail have done things that they don't know they did; they were in a blackout. They were told they did this crazy thing, but they don't remember. Some people get to experience the miserable hell of staying out there the rest of their lives, never finding recovery. Tons of people need recovery and never get it. They have to want it. There are still people who do interventions, but often that's the family being ready, and the family wanting the person to be ready. The person, him or herself, has to be ready.

Sometimes people wanting to help can create even more damage. I had to hit my rock bottom, and there were several of them. If people had stepped in and helped me when they thought I needed help – when I called people begging for money and favors – they'd have prevented me from hitting my bottom. I needed to have the spiritual experience of, *I can't do this any more, I need help.* Just making that statement, "There's a problem here," is part of the solution. Immediately. There's honesty, there's hope, there's faith. It's an acknowledgment that what I have done in the past doesn't work. On the lowest of levels, I have hope that it can change. Once people come to that point, there are tons of resources available now. You just can't be in a city like San Francisco or LA or anywhere today and say, "There's nothing out there to help me." If you want help, it's there. But you have to genuinely want the help.

If you have loved ones out there that you'd like to help, consider looking at yourself and getting yourself some help. Maybe in that seeking there's some finding. Those of you who took time to read this book, you get to be the ones to become more aware of something. You get to be the ones to change. Just like Gandhi said, "Be the change you wish to see in the world." Maybe by your changing, it will help this other person see something isn't quite right with their lifestyle, and make them want to change. Maybe with some help and support for yourself, for the first time you'll be able to say "No." Or, "Yes, actually, it does bother me when you drink and when you use. It affects our relationship, it affects our kids, it affects our neighbors, it affects the safety of others when you drive, it affects me when you hit me and blame it on the alcohol or the drugs."

In yoga, when I teach challenging poses, people come up to me afterward and say, "I didn't know I could do that!" Sometimes I respond, "I didn't know you could either." I've found out people are strong. It's the same thing in recovery. Watching people finally get it is amazing. It reminds me not to underestimate people's courage and strength. Look at what I put my body through, and I'm still alive. Some people do one line of coke and they're dead that very first time they try it. Some people drink too many energy drinks and they're dead. I'm sure there's someone at SF General who's flat lining right now. For some reason I got to live. I attribute most of that to my Higher Power looking out for me oh-so-many times when I couldn't look out for myself.

It is so worth it to be clean and sober. My alternative is that I would have been dead. I'd have missed out on all of this. It's not like my life is everything I want it to be; I've gone through experiences that make me think, *Seriously? Do I really have to go through this?* But, I feel healthy, I get a good night's sleep most nights, and I get to practice yoga. I love yoga. I have friends. I have people who ask me how I'm doing and actually care about the answer. Given where I've been, that alone is amazing. I have Joe. He and I are about to sell everything and move to Bali, one of the most amazing, sacred places on the planet for us.

I'm not unique, I'm garden variety. If I can do it, anyone can. I've seen people with unbelievable reasons why they shouldn't have been able to recover, change or transform, who are living amazing lives now. I didn't do any good deed to get the life I have now. I didn't show up to church and give away all my worldly possessions or dedicate my life to service to get the gift of recovery. Anybody can do it. Anybody can have this gift. There are still some days when I'm not happy I am an alcoholic or an addict, but every day I am grateful that I am one in recovery.

It took a long time to stop blaming others for the love I wasn't getting and to learn how to love myself. If you'd told me that was a possibility before I got here, I'd have laughed in your face. In recovery, we share amazing outcomes if we do the work. If we are diligent about completing the process we will be amazed by the results. That is a gift. Freedom and happiness will begin to show up in our lives, and we will no longer be plagued by our past. We will finally understand peace and serenity. No matter how far we have fallen, we will discover that our experience helps others, and our illusions and delusions of uselessness and self-pity will fade away. Our attitude and perception on life will change as we slowly transition from selfishness to selflessness. Our fear of people and our financial worries will melt away. We will intuitively know how to handle situations that would have caused us to stumble in the past. We will recognize that a Higher Power is effectively doing for us what we tried over and over to do for ourselves. These teachings suggest that they are not over-the-top or extravagant.

For years, I would laugh at the description of these outcomes and dismiss them; at that time, I wasn't doing the work required to get the results. When I heard them, I would always have the same thought, *This can't happen for me, these outcomes are huge. They are very over-the-top and extravagant. Maybe others can achieve them, but for a guy like me, they're ridiculous.* As the group discussed the outcomes I would sit there quietly, not wanting to discourage the new folks with my judgments.

Now, after years of actual work, practice, and trust, when we discuss these outcomes, tears come to my eyes, because they have all been fulfilled in my life. I have worked so hard for them, and I continue to do the work even when my ego resists. These outcomes are all the things I ever wanted to hold in my heart. I mistakenly thought I would attain them by holding onto more and more things in my hands. They came about in the exact opposite way as how I'd tried to get happiness and love into my life in the past. People told me go feed the homeless, go quit your job, go take a yoga teacher training - and I did. Because of all the work I've done, on and off the mat, I get to experience these outcomes as they manifest in my life. And to me, they *are* wildly extravagant. But, that's just one alcoholic's and drug addict's opinion and experience.